WATERFOWL DECOYS OF MICHIGAN AND THE LAKE ST. CLAIR REGION

BLOOMFIELD TOWNSHIP PUBLIC LIBRARY
BLOOMFIELD HILLS, MICHIGAN 48013

WATERFOWL DECOYS OF MICHIGAN AND THE LAKE ST. CLAIR REGION

COLLECTED AND EDITED BY CLUNE WALSH, JR., AND LOWELL G. JACKSON • PHOTOGRAPHY BY BILL JOHNSON

GALE GRAPHICS • BOOK TOWER • DETROIT, MICHIGAN 48226

Copyright © 1983 by Clune Walsh, Jr.

Manufactured and first published in the U.S.A.

Library of Congress Cataloging in Publication Data

Main entry under title:

Waterfowl decoys of Michigan and the Lake St. Clair
  Region.

  Includes index.
   1. Decoys (Hunting)--Michigan. 2. Decoys (Hunting)
--Saint Clair, Lake, Region (Mich. and Ont.)
3. Waterfowl in art. I. Walsh, Clune. II. Jackson,
Lowell G. III. Johnson, Bill, 1931-   .
NK9712.W37   1983   745.593   83-14023
ISBN 0-8103-4243-X
ISBN 0-8103-4244-8 (collector's ed.)
ISBN 0-8103-4245-6 (presentation ed.)

Dedicated to my son Clune J. Walsh III and Phyllis Ellison whose love, excitement, and sense of history for Michigan's singular art form are the cause for this unique book.

1. Widgeon in feeding pose by Dr. Miles Pirnie, waterfowl expert from Michigan State University.

*The hunter crouches in his blind
'Neath camouflage of every kind,
And conjures up a quacking noise
To lend allure to his decoys.
This grown-up man, with pluck
   and luck,
Is hoping to outwit a duck.*

— OGDEN NASH

CONTENTS

	List of Color Plates	x
	Foreword	xii
	Acknowledgments	xvi
	Introduction 　　Donal C. O'Brien, Jr.	xviii
1.	Hunting the Art in Decoys 　　Julie Hall and Michael Hall	2
2.	Nate Quillen (1839-1908) 　　Bernard W. Crandell	14
3.	Unger Decoys 　　Ronald S. Swanson	20
4.	John Schweikart (1870-1954) 　　Julie Hall	24
5.	James R. Kelson (1888-1968) 　　Jerry Catana	32
6.	Ralph Reghi (1914-　) 　　Len Carnaghi	36
7.	The Unusual Decoys of Ferdinand Bach (1888-1967) 　　Edward T. deNavarre and Hal Sorenson	42
8.	Peterson, Dodge, and Mason: 　　The Commercial Makers of Detroit 　　Bernard W. Crandell	48
9.	Tom Schroeder (1885-1976) 　　Ronald S. Swanson	72
10.	Ben Schmidt (1884-1968) 　　William J. Mackey, Jr.	80
11.	Club Carvers 　　Bernard W. Crandell	88
12.	Other Carvers	104
13.	Other Decoys	110
	Index	158

2. Canada goose by Butch Schramm, New Baltimore, c. 1945.

Plate 1	Rare blue goose and two sizes of Canada goose decoys by Ben Schmidt.
Plates 2-3	John Schweikart's dramatic decoys: Four canvasbacks and two whistlers.
Plates 4-5	A variety of Tom Schroeder's best gunning decoys. From left: Bluebill, ringbill, redhead, little bluewing and greenwing teal, pair of ruddy ducks, canvasback, mallard drake.
Plates 6-7	Mason factory decoys. From left: Mallard pair, coot, widgeon, pintail drake, bluewing teal, canvasback.
Plate 8	Classic canvasback decoys by Ralph Reghi.
Plate 9	St. Clair Flats swan decoy. This type is extremely rare.
Plate 10	Nate Quillen decoys. Pair of redheads (above). Extremely rare bluewing teal (below).
Plate 11	Classic Mason shorebird decoys.
Plates 12-13	Group of the Canada Club's best goose decoys.
Plates 14-15	Gunning decoys by Ben Schmidt. From left: Widgeon, canvasback, pintail hen, bluebill, mallard hen, pintail drake, greenwing teal drake.
Plate 16	Decoys by Wells, Warin, and Chambers: Mallards, canvasbacks, and a pintail (above). Rare Tom Chambers wood duck (below).

LIST OF COLOR PLATES

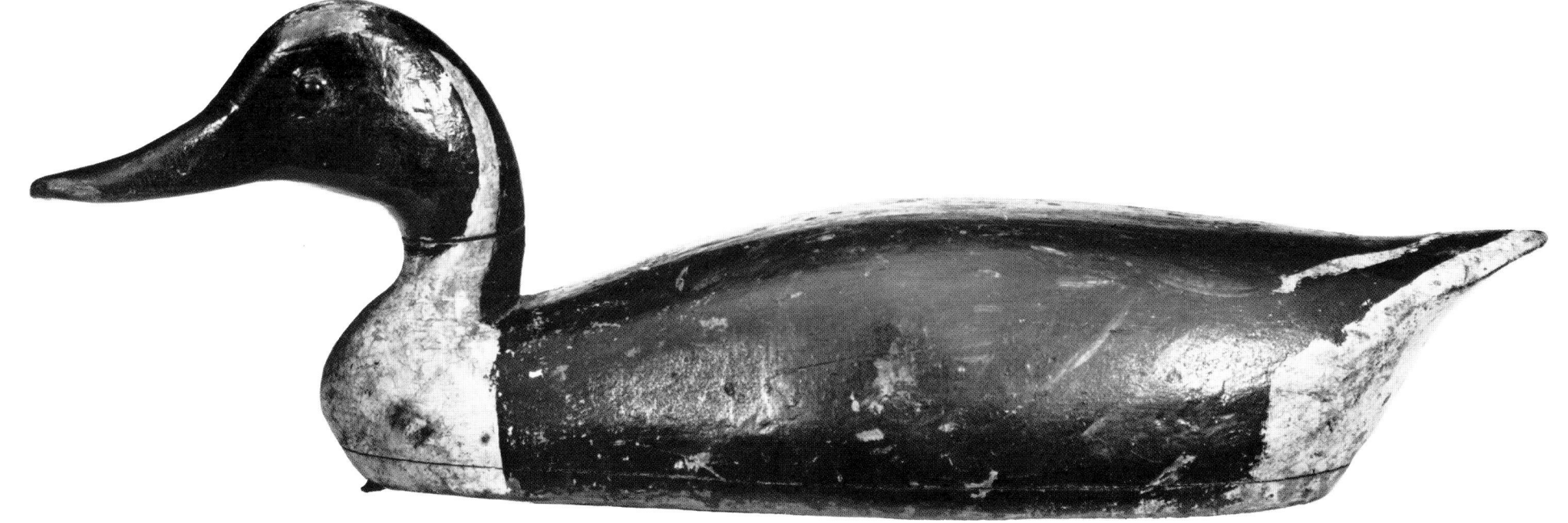

3. Chris Smith carved this unusual pintail, early 1900s.

FOREWORD

If it had not been for the interest of my son Clune in decoys, I might not have become so deeply involved in decoy collecting as I did and as I still am.

In 1971, when Clune was in his twelfth year, my cousin Connie gave him as a Christmas gift William Mackey's *American Bird Decoys*. It was the beginning of his interest in the subject. Because it was, at the time, his only interest, I promptly made it mine. In doing so I learned for the first time that those wooden objects about which I knew so little had an exciting background related not just to hunting but to American folk art.

As Clune and I investigated the subject more deeply, we made the acquaintance of Phyllis Ellison, a Southfield, Michigan, collector, and, under her direction, began spending Saturdays and Sundays exploring collectors' basements. We gradually accumulated our own spread of decoys which, as of this writing, covers not only my basement, but most of the rooms of my house.

Suddenly names like Schweikart, Reghi, Warin, McDonald, and Chambers began to hold for me special significance. I learned with delight that Ralph Reghi and Hank Walters were still active in hunting and guiding, so I sought them out, made their acquaintance, and spent hours in their company fascinated with their recollections. Clune and I also met with carver Tom Schroeder who was ninety-one at the time and in failing health. Butch Schramm was no longer carving but still tended his boat and bait shop at Decker's Landing in St. Clair Flats.

4. Hollow bufflehead drake—the only one known—by Irving Malinski.

These men were the last remaining links with a portion of American history and folk art which had known such meager recording. As I added to my collection, therefore, I added also whatever bits of information I came upon and, in so doing, developed the concept of this book—for which, I became increasingly convinced, a definite need existed.

It was Phyl Ellison who first called to my attention the uniqueness and particular artistry of the Michigan decoy. As my store of information on decoys grew, so did my conviction that the book I was contemplating should center on the phenomenon of so many varied styles of carving emanating from so limited a geographic area. With few exceptions, the decoys appearing in the pages of this book originated in the 45-mile distance from the St. Clair Flats through Lake St. Clair to the delta of the Detroit River. Quillen and the bobtail carvers were downriver. Schweikart, Schroeder, Wallach, Reghi, Bach, Unger, McDonald, and Kelson all hunted in the immediate area. Chambers, Warin, Wells, Reeves, and Ward were only across the South Channel. And Detroit, of course, in the heyday of market hunting, was the home of Mason, Peterson, and the Dodge factory decoys. The locals preferred their own rigs to the rolling Mason, which undoubtedly accounts for the particular and distinctive style of their carving. What accounts for the artistry that invariably went into their work is as difficult to explain as the phenomenon of folk art itself. It is simply there to be valued and enjoyed.

In assembling this book I have called on the knowledge and talents of a number of individuals. While I conceived the book, they have made it what it is. Because it is, therefore, more theirs than it is mine, I can look on it with a degree of detachment that allows me to find it a notable and singular contribution to the field of decoy literature. It is my hope—indeed it is my conviction—that it will carry into the future a worthy account of a period in the history of both hunting and folk art that merits the kind of attention its exceptionally competent carvers have given it in the pages that follow.

Clune J. Walsh, Jr.

5. Pre-Civil War lowhead bufflehead found on the South Channel.

This book is the result of the efforts and encouragement of many friends and collectors. First among these supporters are Phyllis Ellison and Adelle Earnest, who sparked and fanned the idea of a "Michigan book." My most talented father-in-law, Walter Weir, contributed many constructive suggestions for the format and proofread the manuscript in its several stages. And a very special thank you to the following people, who so generously allowed items in their collections to be photographed. Without their help, this display of unique decoys would not have been possible.

Jim Aikin	Frank Cummings
William Beardslee	Ed deNavarre
Ed Bowman, M.D.	Michael & Julie Hall
Len Carnaghi	James Kane, D.D.S.
Jerry Catana	Hank Kotynski
Conrad Clippert	David McKeenan
Joseph Cote	David Potts
Michael Cotter	Ronald S. Swanson
Barney Crandell	George Van Walleghem

ACKNOWLEDGMENTS

Plate 1

Plates 2-3

Plates 4-5

Plates 6-7

Plate 8

Plate 9

Plate 10

Plate 11

Plates 12-13

Plates 14-15

Plate 16

6. Swan of unknown origin used at St. Clair Flats Shooting Co., early 1900s.

INTRODUCTION

by Donal C. O'Brien, Jr.

Picture a gigantic hourglass, the upper wide end stretching across the Great Lakes, tightening to receive the fall migration of North American waterfowl heading south from the summering grounds in Saskatchewan, Manitoba, and Ontario, then spilling out across the Mississippi and Atlantic flyways. Imagine expanses of marshes, interlaced with creeks, pot holes, and bays. It helps now if you are a waterman, but close your eyes and visualize reed-fringed lakes, swift moving canals large enough to carry barges and freighters, and then think of big water—big as any on which ocean gunners set out for waterfowl.

The neck of the hourglass is the area which this book addresses. There are few, if any, areas in North America which provide such accessible hunting for such a large number and variety of ducks and geese. Furthermore, no area of such relatively small size contains such a wide range of waters on which to hunt. These factors have contributed to the rich and remarkable heritage of decoys produced by the decoy makers of Michigan and the St. Clair Flats.

The ideal nature of this area for hunting did not escape the attention of the market gunners or sportsmen, and the decoy makers responded by the middle of the nineteenth century to give folk art collectors some of the earliest and finest examples of wildfowl decoys. Because the waters of and surrounding Lake St. Clair and Lake Erie were the staging grounds for a great variety of waterfowl, the decoy makers of this area produced a full range of diving and marsh duck decoys. In this respect they differed from the makers of other great waterfowl areas where a few species of waterfowl tended to predominate.

7. Canada goose, two-legged stickup from Wallaceburg, Ontario.

The variety of hunting conditions made it necessary for the makers to know the particular bodies of water on which their decoys were to be used and to design them accordingly. Thus for waters within a short distance of each other, these carvers produced, on the one hand, the graceful and delicate birds of the protected marshes of the flats and, on the other, the bold and rugged decoys that were used on the open water of the lakes. On the Atlantic flyway one would have to go all the way from the sea duck decoys of coastal Maine to the Delaware River decoys to find such a contrast. In Michigan it was just across a bay.

I happened to come at decoys from all sides—a love of waterfowl, an ardent interest in gunning and decoy making, and an admiration for the decoy as an art form. The result is an irrevocable intertwining that makes it impossible for me to separate or quantify what pleases me in decoys. Michigan and St. Clair Flats decoys satisfy in all these respects for they offer variety, likeness to species, superb construction, and wonderful folk art form and paint.

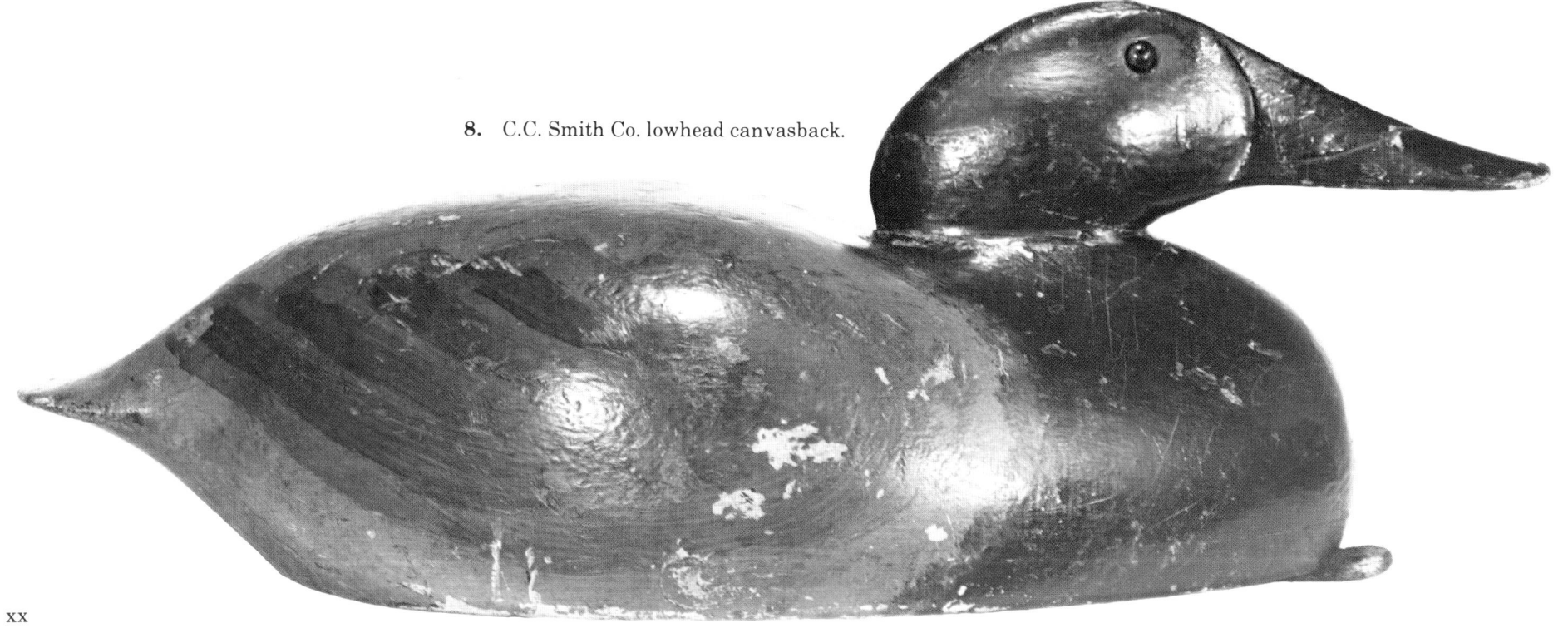

8. C.C. Smith Co. lowhead canvasback.

What rich images are available to the viewer of Michigan and St. Clair Flats decoys—one can imagine how Schweikart might have felt as he looked out on his rig of majestic canvasbacks pulling at anchor on a grey December day, empathize with Tom Chambers as he poled back from a flats pot hole with his crisp and symmetrical mixed rig of marsh ducks and divers stacked in the bow of his boat, share the pleasure and experimentation of John Wells as he completed a pair of shovelers, probably just to have them in his rig, or, if that's your preference, simply sit back and enjoy the unique whimsy of a Quillen redhead, the controlled and easy grace of a Warin goose or pintail, or the beauty of so many other of the great decoys that came out of Michigan and the St. Clair Flats.

9. A classic silhouette. Canvasback decoy (maker unknown) from St. Clair Flats, Michigan.

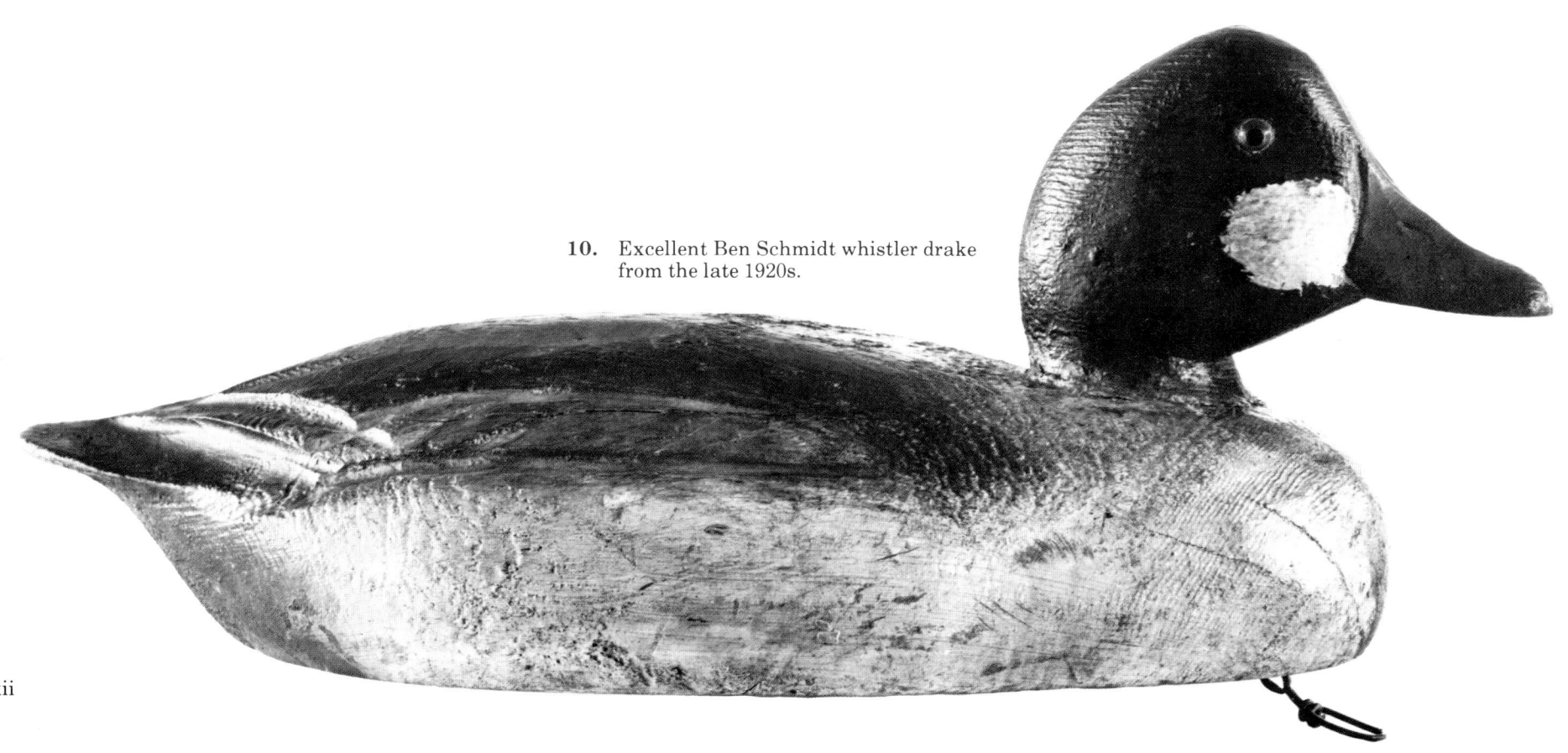

10. Excellent Ben Schmidt whistler drake from the late 1920s.

11. "JRW Maker" goes top grade with this beautiful pintail.

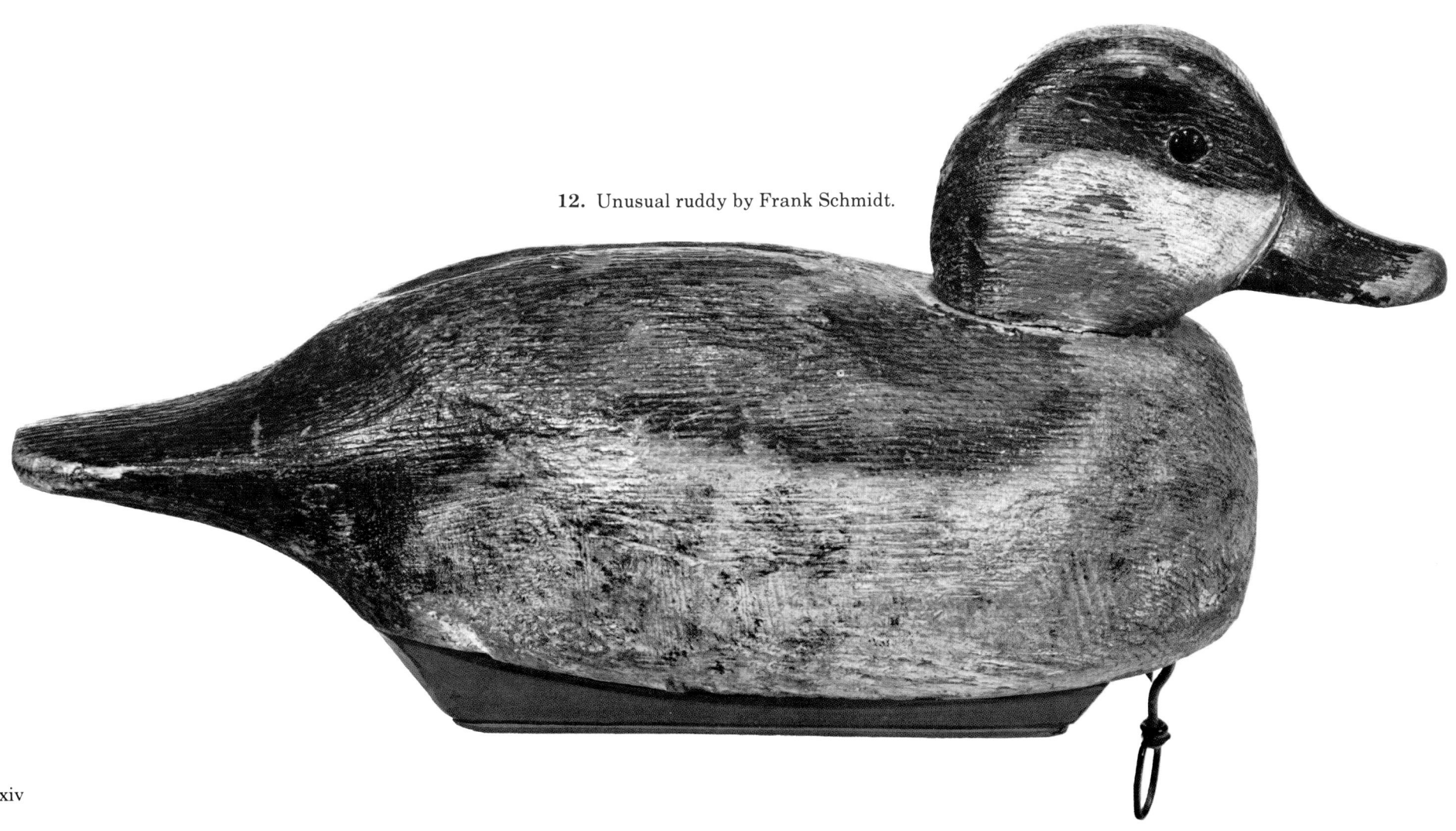

12. Unusual ruddy by Frank Schmidt.

WATERFOWL **DECOYS** OF MICHIGAN AND THE LAKE ST. CLAIR REGION

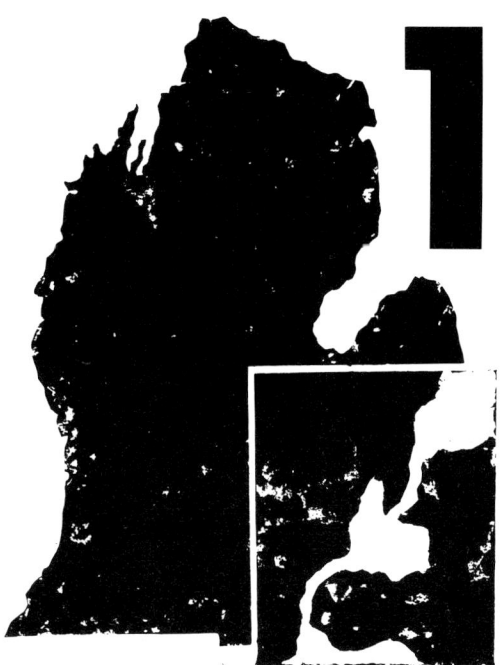

HALL & HALL

CANVASBACK

HUNTING THE ART IN DECOYS
by Julie Hall and Michael Hall

Twelve fine Michigan and Ontario canvasback drakes, needing no superfluous ornamentation to evoke all the artistry and magic of decoys. A dozen decoys, each sharing certain characteristics, yet somehow all so different. Each began as a carved wood portrait of the canvasback duck. As portraits, however, each carving is not only a likeness of a bird, but also a fascinating mirror of the hand and mind that fashioned it. The differences between decoys reflect the fact that no two carvers possess the same creative ideas. When a carver shapes a bird that authoritatively and beautifully expresses his unique vision, he becomes an artist and his work is destined to eventually reach a collector.

Many of the aesthetic principles of decoy carving derived from the formal building blocks basic to all art. Shapes, lines, colors, and textures—the decoy maker organizes these to please his eye and delight his imagination. Part painter and part sculptor—the decoy carver is in many ways the complete artist.

Some carvers are particularly responsive to the quality of line in their art. From any angle the silhouette of George Warin's canvasback (fig. 22) is a fascinating study of curves and angles. The lines of this decoy are without peer. The arc of its back, the edge line of its bill, the curve of its chest, and even the precise outline of its bottom board are a virtuoso performance by a master craftsman.

13. Impressive tin-wing canvasback from the Schweikart rig (used for four generations but still in excellent original paint).

14. Ralph Reghi bullneck.

15. Nice Ben Schmidt can, c. 1952.

Other makers seem more interested in solid shapes and volumes than in lines and profiles. Ralph Reghi's canvasback (fig. 16) epitomizes the traditional notion of decoys as "floating sculpture." This canvasback is easily viewed as a combination of strong geometric shapes. The bird's head is a simple pyramid. The body is an ovaloid solid—the neck a near perfect cylinder. Each shape in this decoy is executed with precision, then carefully blended into the adjacent shape. The completed carving is sculpture—pure and simple.

Still other decoy carvers seem primarily involved with textures and surfaces. Ben Schmidt obviously delighted in doing the rasp work and feather carving which gave his decoys a lifelike appearance and unique tactile appeal (see figure 15). The paint impasto on the Strubing canvasback (figs. 18 and 19) reflects another decoy maker's preoccupation with texture. Strubing's paint, applied in thick patterns of ridges and peaks, brings to mind the rich, sensuous paint surfaces of Lem Ward.

The utilitarian function of the decoy invariably enters into a discussion of what makes decoys collectible. As a hunting lure, the decoy was designed with considerable attention to its function. Serviceability and art, however, are not necessarily the same. Thus the best floating, easiest handling, most practically constructed decoy may not be the best collector's decoy.

Many of the most artistic carvers seem to have unconsciously preferred aesthetic considerations to the practical. The slender necks of the Michigan "bobtail" (fig. 20) are far too thin to be practical on a working decoy. The maker obviously preferred to take his chances

16. Bullneck canvasback by Reghi.

with inevitable breakage rather than sacrifice the lines and proportions of the tiny neck that pleased him aesthetically.

John Schweikart (fig. 13) also ignored practical considerations when he set aluminum wing tips and tail feathers into the backs of his canvasback decoys. The delicate metal shapes undoubtedly caught on hunting gear, bent in handling, and lifted with time and thus required occasional repair. Schweikart happily maintained and repainted his decoys in exchange for the pleasure he received each fall gazing at his carvings from his boat.

The "home grown" sense of style so evident in many decoys has made them attractive to collectors interested in what is often called folk or primitive art. Decoy making clearly qualifies as a folk art, but few decoys are truly primitive art. Collectors all too often brand as primitive those decoys which, though badly made or awkward in appearance, still have some basic charm. A good primitive must be more than charming to be collectible. At its best it should be full of visual surprises, rich in detail, and provide a vigorous challenge to the collector who seeks a touch to all aspects of art.

The Zeke McDonald canvasback (fig. 25) is a primitive. The hollow construction of this decoy indicates that McDonald was not unaware of the local tradition of decoy making around him in the St. Clair Flats, yet his image of a canvasback is highly original. The great head on his can rises on its slim neck like a giant lollipop on a stick. The broad oversized bill juts out from the bird's face like a snow plow blade. The decoy's body is flat and simple but it is punctuated with a beautiful tiny tail that gives the whole carving a sense of style. As art, the McDonald canvasback has both the originality and authority that make a good, collectible primitive.

For most of the old-time makers, a subconscious need to capture the spirit of a bird in a carving clearly outstripped any conscious intention to produce a mere photographic bird likeness. As outdoorsmen and hunters, most of the old-timers knew the habits, moods, and personalities of wild birds and often vitalized their decoys with a pose or posture that captures a particular essence of life. There is no decoy collector who has not been moved by the decoy which in the thrust of its neck or the cock of its head is transformed into something more than a wooden duck.

The anonymous maker of the St. Anne's Club sleeper (fig. 27) focused the essence of

watchfulness in the eyes of his resting bird. Content in pose but wary in spirit, this simple abstract carving mirrors what its author knew of the patient vigilance so necessary to the wild canvasback's survival. Carl Wallach saw the canvasback (fig. 21) as the regal king of the flyways. His bobtail sentinel seems indomitable—arrogant and almost indifferent to the hazards of migration. Puffed up and confident, this decoy reflects a carver's respect for the wild birds he sought to lure to his gun.

The "snaky-head" can (fig. 17) is another matter altogether. This bird is restless, nervous, and very wild. Curiously, in dubbing this decoy the "snaky-head," Michigan collectors have unconsciously recalled the evolution of birds from reptiles. The reptilian aspect of this decoy

17. Unusual snaky-head, flat-bodied, hollow canvasback from the St. Clair Flats.

18. Walter Strubing of Marine City made this hollow, oversized, classic can.

19. Majestic canvasback by Strubing. Unique paint pattern is a Strubing trademark.

20. Bobtailed canvasback, maker unknown. Note pinched neck style.

21. Bobtailed canvasback, the work of Carl Wallach.

22. Classic canvasback by George Warin.

23. Chambers canvasback with fine comb painting.

24. Chambers canvasbacks like this sold for $70 a dozen, an unheard of price 70 years ago.

25. Zeke McDonald: hollow canvasback drake.

is strangely compelling, leaving little doubt as to why both birds and snakes have figured so prominently in man's myths and legends since the dawn of time.

What then is the limit? What constitutes the perfect decoy? Tom Chambers was working on the perfect decoy in 1910. This Canadian craftsman produced a canvasback (fig. 24) of extraordinary grace and subtlety. Alert but gentle, this decoy is an elegant study of classic shapes and profiles enriched by an eccentric chest line and a slight turn of its head. The beauty of this carving is its quiet presence. Chambers's artistic statement approaches a limit of understatement that perfectly embodies his vision.

John Zachmann is working on the perfect decoy today. His 1974 sleeper (fig. 26) is a powerful composition of bold forms and incisive lines. The bird's massive head turns and lays flat against its back, creating a tight play of interlocked sculptural shapes. The carving ripples with the sense of toned muscles bulging under skin and feathers. Nature as power—the canvasback duck as a migration machine.

The perfect decoy is not one bird but rather all the great decoys that have ever been found and all the rest that wait to be discovered. In art there is no single "right" way. The artist finds his way and waits for others to discover the verity of his design. Decoy making is a folk craft production with a long history. Decoy collecting is a search for the results of those occasions when vision and craft synthesized magnificently. A dozen decoys is only a beginning—twelve spots in the intricate patchwork of man's artistic legacy. Every great decoy, like every great painting or piece of pottery, provides a window through which man views the best of his own creative potential.

26. Canvasback sleeper by John Zachmann.

27. Sleeper cans from the St. Anne's Club, St. Clair Flats.

NATE QUILLEN (1839-1908)
by Bernard W. Crandell

A century ago Nate Quillen lived near the famed duck marshes of Pointe Mouillee on western Lake Erie. He was a locksmith, a cabinetmaker, a boat builder, and a decoy-maker. Still another profession of Quillen's was the seasonal one of guiding or "punting" at the Pointe Mouillee Shooting Club in the late 1800s. Locksmithing, cabinetmaking, and punting aside, the Quillen talents that are in evidence and worthy of historical note today are his decoys and his boats. While many of his monitors and punt boats are still in use, most of his decoys have found their way to collectors' shelves throughout the country.

The late decoy historian Joel Barber was so captivated by the Quillen lowhead that upon acquiring his first, he proceeded to satisfy his architectural instincts by pulling off the bottom board in order to make a cross-section drawing of the unique construction. Because of Quillen's original craftsmanship, his birds have been recognized as highly desirable examples of perfectionism in the decoy-maker's art and they have drawn praise from decoy collectors across the country.

Michigan collectors who "discovered" Quillen describe with justifiable pride the Quillen lowhead redheads as undeniably outstanding examples of the kind of product that could only come from a perfectionist cabinetmaker. Quillen not only hollowed out the bodies but the heads of these tiny birds as well, making them weigh less than a pound apiece. Quillen inletted the head and neck into the body with such precision that the seams are still tight

28. Nate Quillen redhead and bluebill in his boat-body style.

29. Quillen boat-body redhead in super condition (used at Long Point Company in Port Rowan, Ontario).

today after more than 80 years of water, wear, and weather.

Another feature of this decoy's head was its contour, which easily fit the hunter's hand. It could be grabbed with no slippage, and so the wrapping of the anchor line was hastened.

While the lowheads are a classic decoy style and perhaps the most popular Quillen decoy among collectors, the standard high-necks of many species came from the Quillen workshop with just as much care and precision.

30. Quillen lowhead redheads. Masterpieces from the late 1800s.

Quillen's shop, adjacent to his small frame house, included a saw mill for rough-cutting logs and all the tools of a master carpenter and locksmith. He was as meticulous in the preparation of the wood as he was in his carving. According to James N. Foote, Jr., an ardent collector of Quillen lore, Quillen first dried the Michigan white cedar logs for a year in his barn.

"Then he rough-cut the logs into sizes suitable for decoys and put them back into the barn to dry another year," Foote relates. "After finishing the carving of the decoy, he dried it for another complete year before painting! Any splitting or other imperfection that showed up during the three years of seasoning eliminated the block from production."

Quillen also made the heads of cedar. He did not use any lead keels or weights, although many of these have been added by the users.

Quillen made both hollow decoys, which he sold to the Pointe Mouillee Club members for one dollar, and solid decoys when knots in the wood prevented hollowing. He sold the solid decoys to local gunners for twenty-five cents. He was a prolific carver. The best estimate of Quillen's production rate was about 200 annually. His most productive years apparently were from 1875 to 1900, when the demand for his decoys was high.

Quillen species include redheads, canvasbacks, bluebills, ruddys, buffleheads, pintails, widgeon, blacks and mallards; occasionally, a blue-wing teal has been found.

The hollows, models of superb craftsmanship, have one small drawback as collectors' items. Quillen's aesthetic sense made him carve the necks (excepting the lowheads) with a slim, graceful realism that could not stand the rough treatment on the marsh. Thus many of the decoys existing today have cracked necks. Quillen did, however, use a metal screw up through the necks and heads which prevented them from coming apart.

The practice of making the head and neck as one unit and inletting it into the body had its practical advantages. True, it was a time-consuming feat of fine carpentry, but if there was head damage, the unit could be quickly removed and a spare inserted with a minimum of repair time. Heads on the lowhead decoys and on the long-necks are interchangeable with remarkably close tolerances.

A source of Quillen history was the late William T. Barbour of Bloomfield Hills, a Pointe Mouillee Club member for many years beginning in 1896. He wrote a history of the club in 1922, recalling Quillen as "an artist as well as an artisan."

"He took great pride in the work he did," Barbour noted. "As models for his decoys he used birds that were shot in the marsh. He was very neat, and everything had to be in perfect order. Not only would he make the decoys but he also painted them, and every bit of color was applied with great exactness and care. . . . His appearance and temperament were those of an artist."

With the closing of the Pointe Mouillee Club in 1944, the State of Michigan acquired the property and moved the old buildings. Many boats and decoys owned by the ten members were sold to Edward Lezotte, a guide at the club, and Felix Zembke, the club superintendent.

Since each member owned roughly 500 decoys, consisting primarily of Quillens and Masons, there still, obviously, was a wonderful wealth of Quillen decoys for collectors as late as 1960.

Lezotte bought the rigs of several members and turned the decoys to good use. He ran the state's boat rental concession at Pointe Mouillee for fourteen years, also renting out mixed Quillens and Mason decoys to hunters at a daily rate of $1.25 per dozen. Some hunters, however, replaced rented decoys with broken old clunkers, taking home the good ones. Lezotte finally had to inspect every bag of decoys as they were turned in. That these decoys, stored in wet burlap bags on a dirt floor, alternately freezing and thawing season after season, ever survived is a tribute to the fine Quillen craftsmanship.

Lezotte stored approximately 500 Quillens and Masons in the Department of Conservation garage at Pointe Mouillee. They were all lost in 1955 when the garage caught fire and burned to the ground.

Although most of the other Quillen decoys found their way to collectors in the 1960s, occasionally one can still be found in a hunting rig, as Jim Foote relates: "I was walking past a duck hunter's boat on a trailer in the Pointe Mouillee parking lot and saw a dozen Quillen lowheads in the boat. I went into the office where the hunter was obtaining his shooting permit and asked if he would like to trade the old decoys for some new ones. 'Sure,' the hunter replied. 'Them damn squatters are bad ones. If you shoot a hole in them, they leak, anyhow!'" The deal was consummated on the spot.

Many boat builders in the lower Detroit River area have tried to copy Quillen's duck hunting boats, but none could match his standards of craftsmanship.

No decoy makers have been known to copy Quillen's decoys. The fine carpentry and the hours needed to turn out his little masterpieces are, perhaps, too much for another carver to face.

31. Quillen widgeon drake, rear, and redhead drake with contrasting body styles.

32. Quillen's pintail was one of his most dramatic decoys (above and left).

SWANSON 3

UNGER DECOYS
by Ronald S. Swanson

Some of the earliest decoys and best decoys to have emanated from the American side of the Flats area were produced by two German families—the Ungers and the Schweikarts. The two families emigrated from Germany to Detroit in the late 1850s. It is evident from a study of their decoys and the locations of their homes and hunting lodges that they carved and hunted together and combined to create some of the most interesting decoys of the area. Whether the Ungers and the Schweikarts originated the Flats style of decoy or whether they were influenced by George Warin's Walpole style is a point that probably will never be adequately covered to anyone's satisfaction—but they must take a great deal of credit for "grandfathering" the American carvers.

The Schweikart family was by far the more prominent and a lot of its history has been uncovered, while little has been found to indicate an accurate record of the Ungers. What is known about the Ungers, however, is that Charles J. Unger was established in Detroit in 1858 as a ship's carpenter and he remained in that profession as an independent until he died in 1881 at the age of 62. His son Frederick C. (1851-1925) was established as a cigar manufacturer as early as 1870 until an apparent semiretirement in 1916. It was Fred who laid claim to and built a hunting cottage on Unger's Island on the south side of the mouth of the Middle Channel in 1895. But because of the obvious great age of the few collected Unger decoys and the father's skill as a carpenter, we assume that Charles made some of the decoys. The possibility is that they worked on them together because the brand "UNGER" is found

33. Unger canvasback.

on some bottom boards rather than a more specific brand such as "CHAS J. UNGER" or "F.C. UNGER".

The Unger decoys were probably made in the period of 1865-1881. If, however, Fred had been solely responsible for them, they would be dated slightly later. An assumption on dating decoys is made here: in most cases decoy carvers, who were sportsmen or market hunters, got started early and produced their first good hunting rigs in their twenties or thirties. This is supported by the fact that the Detroit/Lake St. Clair area was heavily oriented towards fishing and wildfowling from the Civil War's end to the mid-1930s and most men learned these sports as teenagers. Also, there were few, if any, good professional decoy carvers prior to 1900 on the American side. It is true that Dodge and Mason decoys were available as early as the 1880s, but these decoys were expensive and singularly unpopular with the redhead and can hunters of the Flats area because they pitched and rolled excessively. The serious hunter had to turn his own hand to create a good hunting rig—and the lightweight, hollow, flat-bottomed "Flats style" was the result. Unger decoys are important not only because of their age but also because of their technical superiority, and the influence passed on by their design.

Unger decoys appear to have been made for a private rig as only a few (less than 25) have been found. Cans and redheads stamped "UNGER" and three or four unmarked black ducks have been found. Only one known decoy remains in original paint and this redhead (see figure 35) is testimony to Unger's exceptional skill as a carver as well as an extremely competent painter.

34. Unger black and canvasback. Early decoys dramatizing the tail differences between a diver and a puddle duck.

35. Redhead decoy branded "UNGER" from Harsen's Island in 1880 (also above).

There are two basic styles of Unger decoys. The earlier style is long and narrow and may have been done by Charles. The later, wider style is probably the work of Fred. Whether the early or the late, Unger decoys have many unique characteristics in common. Probably the most noticeable is the very small eyes which were either taxidermist-style glass eyes, or black beads. A very unusual but less noticeable characteristic is that many of the divers have hollow heads. These have been carefully augered out from the front under the chin and hollowed; then the hole was covered with a thin piece of cork. Uniquely, the under side of the bills are also gouged out on a number of decoys in an effort to reduce head weight and lower the center of gravity in order to produce the most stable decoy possible. The head and bill carving is carefully done, accurately depicting the species through a great variety of head positions. (The variations all fall within the straight forward position—no sleepers or turned heads are known.) The bodies of the cans and redheads are very smooth, turtle-backed decoys with a small low tail. Unger black ducks are very rare, but they are easily identified by their high up sweeping stern sections and small eyes. All the decoys are extremely lightweight and have been referred to as "egg shell" decoys. The later style is much wider, gaining visibility and lateral stability at only a small sacrifice in weight.

It is almost impossible to find two Unger decoys that are identical. This is not because of poor craftsmanship on the part of the maker, but must be credited to artistry, because all the slight variations from bird to bird combine to give a very lifelike appearance and sense of movement to the rig. This valuable characteristic is more in the style of rigs from Monhegan and Cobb's Island and Stratford than in rigs from Barnegat, the Chesapeake, or the Delaware River.

The painting of Unger decoys is difficult to be definite about because most of them have been found in poor condition. The one exception, the mint redhead already mentioned, shows clearly, however, that his painting style was bold and expressive, not tight and patterned like many decoy painters. A stipple effect was used on the back of the decoy to reduce glare and the colors were very close to the birds the rig was designed to lure.

However, as far as one can tell, his black ducks received less attention. They were painted a dark gray-black except for the light olive bills, and there was no special effort put into the lighter areas on the sides of the head and neck. On the other hand, some of the canvasbacks show faint evidence of very fine comb-painting for the original coat.

All in all, Unger decoys must be rated among the best of the Flats decoys, a distinction which, until recently, has not been made because of their rarity and the poor condition in which they have been found.

JOHN SCHWEIKART
(1870-1954)
by Julie Hall

Decoy buffs argue for hours over just what constitutes a great decoy. Some admire graceful lines and will be readily attracted to the geese of Joe Lincoln. Others seek the distinctive eccentricities of form that give character and personality to the cans and ruddys of Lem Dudley. Still others respond to the pensive air of mystery that Nathan Cobb could impart to a chunk of spar in transforming it into a swimming brant.

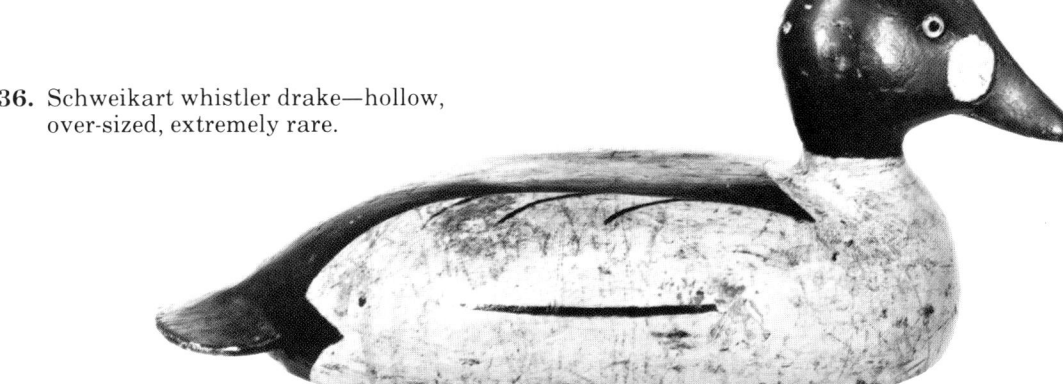

36. Schweikart whistler drake—hollow, over-sized, extremely rare.

The roster of great decoys must now include the carvings of John Schweikart. The recent discovery of a complete Schweikart rig finally supports the claims of greatness made by the collectors fortunate enough to have found occasional Schweikart birds over the years.

Schweikart decoys seem to have it all. There is grace in the line of their backs and wings. There is uniqueness to their shape and construction, and no one confronting a Schweikart can ignore the enigmatic presence of the carving as it "watches" from the shelf. All Schweikarts have a special and elusive quality that makes them stand out. They have that unexplainable "something" that invites debate and ultimately puts Schweikart in the ranks of the Cobbs, Wards, and Walkers that have made decoy history.

At the turn of the century, the Schweikart rig was bringing birds to the gun in the marsh waters around Strawberry Island in the St. Clair Flats. Anyone who has studied the decoys of the Flats recognizes two very distinctive schools of carving found in the area. The first is generally referred to as the Toronto School, and includes decoys used in the Canadian hunt clubs located in the eastern sector of Lake St. Clair. These carvings are delicate, light, symmetrical, and exquisitely crafted. They bear a remarkable school similarity to each other, and trace their genealogies to such notable Canadian carvers as the Warins, the Reeves family, J.R.W., and Thomas Chambers. The second school includes a group of American carvers who were based on the western shore of the lake in and around the town of Mt. Clemens, Michigan. This school, though not so clearly identifiable as the Toronto School, emerges, nonetheless, as a distinct tradition. The Mt. Clemens carvers made birds which were large, direct, and awkwardly impressive. The genesis of this bold style can now be traced out of Mt. Clemens and east across a few miles of open water to Strawberry Island, and to the hands of John Schweikart.

The bullneck style of canvasback associated with such fine Mt. Clemens carvers as Wallach, Kelson, and Reghi clearly originated in the Schweikart rig. The Schweikart influence is seen everywhere in the Flats, indicating that this one man's artistry had a ripple effect that spread across time to touch even such late carvers as Ferdinand Bach. Schweikart decoys predate almost all other Flats carvings by known Michigan makers. The impact of these birds on decoy making in the Flats suggests that Schweikart was, in some ways, to Michigan carving what Albert Laing was to Connecticut decoy carving.

The Schweikart rig included bluebills, redheads, canvasbacks, whistlers, and some of the most interesting coots ever to hit the water. Schweikart's bluebills and redheads are simple carvings with small necks and aggressive heads. His cans and whistlers are large with massive heads and broad, flat bases. All the carvings are typical Flats in their construction—hollow, with thin bottom boards. Some even have their heads hollowed out to make them even lighter. Whatever the species, all Schweikarts can be easily distinguished from all other decoys found in the St. Clair Flats.

Schweikart cans come with several head positions. There are alert, high-headed sentinels; contented, straight heads with medium-length necks; and a few resting lowheads. The lowheads qualify as highly original works of folk sculpture. Their bodies are simple, flat shapes set with characteristic metal wing tips and topped with a nestling head. The boldly sculptured highhead cans with their tubular bull necks convey the strength, independence, and pride that this maker saw in the ducks he knew and hunted.

37. Bullneck canvasback with aluminum wingtips by Captain John Schweikart, Strawberry Island, St. Clair Flats, c. 1900.

Schweikart carved two sizes of whistlers. The most interesting ones are curiously oversized. Speculation persists as to why these dynamic carvings are so much larger than the live birds they simulate. Perhaps they were used for spring hunting and were oversized in order to be seen above the chunks of ice that choke Lake St. Clair in early spring. Although the reason for their size may never be known, their artistic quality is self-evident. Exaggerating the fat cheeks and pointy topknot of the whistler, Schweikart created a most expressive sculptural form. His lowhead whistler hen sits broodingly silent while the drake holds up his huge head in introverted watchfulness—unmoved, but not unaware of possible danger.

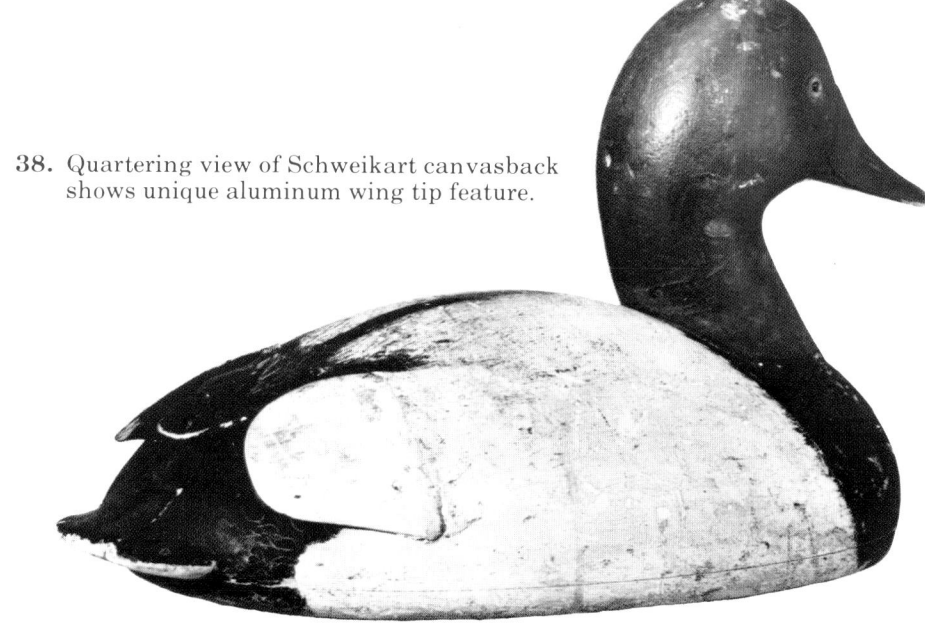

38. Quartering view of Schweikart canvasback shows unique aluminum wing tip feature.

For early Atlantic Flyway carvers, the fantastic color patterns, racy profiles, and varieties of shapes found in mergansers, teal, eiders, and widgeon inspired the production of all sorts of imaginative and highly artistic decoys. Michigan carvers, on the other hand, based their art on the comparatively humble redhead, bluebill, and canvasback. Schweikart's cans prove, once and for all, that the best carvers should be able to find creative inspiration in the commonplace as well as in the exotic.

Many hunters feel that the canvasbacks are the royalty of the game ducks. Schweikart obviously held this sentiment. He portrayed the can as a large, regal bird with a powerful tubular neck and a massive, intelligent head. The delicate shoulders of his cans swell into full, round bodies, which, in turn, recede into flat, authoritative, spade-shaped tails.

Schweikart canvasbacks are notable for one feature that is virtually a trademark. Like Elmer Crowell, Schweikart was fascinated with the problem of incorporating wing tips into the form of a decoy. To solve this problem, he cut stylized crescents and triangles from sheet aluminum and applied them to the back of the carving to create a sense of real wing tips folded over the tail of each carved bird. The aluminum shape was nailed to the body of the bird and blended into the body form with a small amount of filler. Once affixed and blended, the metal details were primed and painted along with the rest of the bird. This ingenious Schweikart innovation is not found on any other known decoy, and must be counted as one of the factors bringing real magic and individuality to this mater's work.

39. A very rare lowhead can by Schweikart.

Schweikart was not a fancy painter. He used paint to complement form. With a simple palette of basic earth colors Schweikart was able to give his birds a rich, soft, feathery surface. Schweikart, like Lem Ward, was challenged by the problem of painting hens, and he reveled in the subtle coloration of the female of each species. His beautiful canvasback hens are a symphony of tans, grays, browns, and chalky white, with each feather pattern wonderfully suggested. These hens blend and contrast with their boldly patterned drakes. Together they make a perfect pair.

40. Schweikart canvasback.

John Schweikart should also be noted for his innovations in decoy hydrodynamics. He fitted some of his decoys with retractable, butterfly-shaped brass keels. These keels, hinged in the middle and cut to the shape of the bottom board of the carvings, were designed to drop down and spread out to stabilize the decoy in the water. Out of the water, they folded flush with the bottom of the bird to simplify handling or storage of the decoy. The turn of a wing nut dropped the two halves of the keel or held them flat to the bottom of the carving.

Schweikart's life is an interesting story itself. His father, Walter, arrived in Detroit, Michigan, from Wizenhausen, Germany, in 1859. Walter was already trained in Germany as a stone-carver and as a woodworker, and he taught his sons many mechanical skills. His family grew to include three sons and two daughters. John, the third son, was born in 1870. The water was always the true home for the Schweikarts and Walter moved his family to Belle Isle, an island situated between Detroit and Windsor, in 1873. Young John and his older brothers, Walter, Jr., and Carl, rowed back and forth to Detroit from school every day until the family returned to the mainland when the city purchased Belle Isle for a park in 1879. The island remains a public park today, and the white clapboard Schweikart home still stands there, serving as an information center for visitors.

By the 1880s Detroit was a busy city. Throughout this era the Schweikart family business, which included an ice company, a commercial fishing venture, and a tavern, all flourished. After a period of prosperity, Walter, Sr., began to search for a remote retreat where he and his sons could escape the city for some fine hunting and quiet. He claimed a tiny island in the Flats and called it Strawberry. Thirteen years after his father's death in 1904, John took ownership of this hunters' paradise for himself.

As a young man John Schweikart worked his way up in all of the family businesses. He is listed in the 1904 Detroit city directory as president of the Schweikart Boat Works. Working with his brother Carl, a master boat builder, John had learned how to work with his hands and continued the family tradition of respect for craftsmanship and pride of workmanship. The aluminum wing tips and special brass hardware found on Schweikart

41. Schweikart redhead.

decoys were clearly made from materials that would have been common around a boat shop. A Schweikart redhead which recently fell from a collector's shelf cracked open to reveal a bold signature on the inside of its bottom board which reads: "John Schweikart—maker/owner—Detroit 1908." It is reasonable to assume that it was at the boat works that John created his wonderful decoys.

As the family's wealth and reputation increased, Carl Schweikart became well known along the Detroit River as the builder of the fastest racing yachts. John sailed these boats, winning numerous races with his personal yacht, *The Huntress*. John was the only one of the Schweikart sons to ever earn the title Captain. Captain John continued to sail *The Huntress* and to shoot over his unique decoys until his death in 1954. Until recently, the decoys were still in use, having excellently served four generations of Schweikarts.

Because Schweikart carved only for his own use as a hunter, the number of birds that left his bench are few compared to the prodigious output of professional carvers like Ira Hudson or Thomas Chambers. The carvings from the one rig that has been found are gathering a strong following among collectors. Local Michigan decoy lore maintains that William Mackey saw and purchased a few Schweikart canvasbacks a year or so before his death, and that Mackey called them his "Captain Cans" and left a standing order for more. Where are these birds today? There was no mention of them in Mackey's writing, and they certainly never showed up in the auction of his estate. We can only speculate. Maybe the great collector traded them quietly to other enthusiasts, or perhaps they reside in the company of the small group of his favorite carvings that remains unaccounted for today.

However, it doesn't take a Mackey to know that these birds are important. The photographs here should illustrate why all Schweikart decoys are memorable. They have originality and honesty without affectation or fussy detail. They have respectable age and have generated that most credible compliment of all—imitation by generations of other carvers. The decoy legacy of John Schweikart adds a new chapter to the story of America's best and most original folk art, and is certain to bring enduring pleasure to collectors everywhere.

42. Schweikart coot.

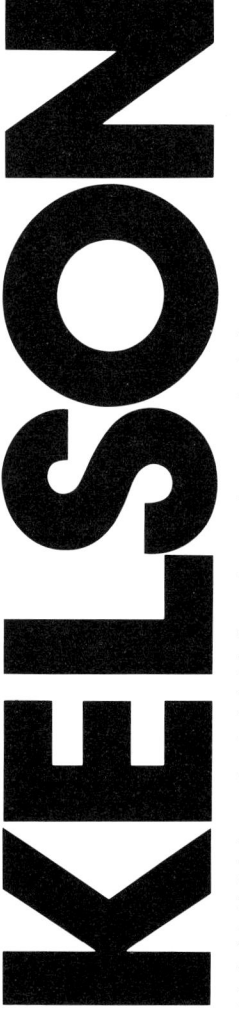

JAMES R. KELSON
(1888-1968)
by Jerry Catana

James R. Kelson was born on August 7, 1888, in Woodstock, Ontario. Some nine years later his family moved to Detroit where Jim, who was fond of the water, became an avid fisherman. Listening to friends talk about duck hunting, he was moved to give it a try, little realizing it would become his way of life. Enthusiastic about his new-found sport, he introduced it to his brother, Malcomb. Equipped with a duck boat and a rig of redhead and canvasback, they ventured onto Lake St. Clair. Here the two boys shot many ducks, selling them for twenty-five cents a pair.

His intense love of life on the lake prompted Jim to quit his shipyard job in 1912, and from that time on he earned his livelihood hunting, fishing, carving decoys, and building boats. He guided for fifteen dollars a day, giving his clients the first twenty-five ducks bagged and keeping the remainder to sell. He soon became an expert guide and craftsman, building duck boats and carving duck and fish decoys. Although Kelson made decoys as early as 1902, no one appears to remember them. A number of people, however, recall his large decoys of the early 1920s, particularly the long thicknecked canvasbacks. These were styled after feeding and carefree birds. They had "heads with a purpose," the long neck serving as a handle for picking up the decoys at the end of a day's hunt. In later rigs, the necks were thinned down and a high back pattern was used to give the decoys a more relaxed appearance.

In 1928, Ralph Reghi, whom Kelson had met a few years earlier as a boy, began carving with Jim and over the years the two developed many carving innovations. Reghi recalls that they did not have a band saw so he and Kelson would cut their stock for bodies and heads with a coping saw. They would then chop the blocks with a hatchet before using a drawknife, spokeshave, and rasp. The heads were carved with a pocketknife. While Reghi sold the decoys he made through a Detroit sporting goods store, Kelson sold only his old shooting rigs which he would then replace.

In 1939 they experimented with balsa, using these decoys in Jim's rig. They had to remove

43. Two Jim Kelson styles are noted in this bluebill, c. 1935, and balsa can sleeper, c. 1957.

them, however, because they skated, sailed with the wind, and rolled in the rough water. Reghi tried a heavier keel but the decoys still caught the wind. Kelson solved the problem by cutting off the top half to give the decoy a low profile that cut down on resistance.

Reghi recollects that he and Kelson made "one hell of a lot of decoys," estimating the total number in the thousands. Following World War II when balsa was in great abundance, they ceased using cedar altogether, having found that balsa provided them with a highly desirable combination—a light decoy with excellent stability that did not have to be hollowed. Kelson died January 12, 1968.

44. Mallard drake by Jim Kelson, fishing and hunting guide who lived on the Clinton River.

45. Mallard hen by Kelson, c. 1925.

46. Turned-head style is displayed in Jim Kelson's balsa redhead (left) and Ralph Reghi's bluebill drake (right). Kelson and Reghi hunted together for many years.

RALPH REGHI (1914-   )
by Len Carnaghi

It is difficult to discuss decoys today without mentioning the name of Ralph Reghi. He is among the last living craftsmen from the golden age of decoy carving. Living in Detroit, Ralph still enjoys reminiscing about his some fifty years as a decoy maker and expert duck hunter.

Ralph Reghi's companions throughout the years read like the *Who's Who* of Michigan decoy carvers. He was closest to the late carver Jim Kelson. Ralph enjoyed a large carving collaboration with Kelson that lasted until Kelson's death in 1968. Ralph also talks freely of his memories of the great Ben Schmidt, Frank Schmidt, Tom Schroeder, Ferdinand Bach, Yock Meldrum, John Schweikart, Pauli Sears, Butch Schramm, Hank Walters, "Pecore" Fox, and so many others from the Michigan area.

In 1967 Ralph met Nick Purdo and John Zachmann and his interest in carving contemporary decoys increased. However, Ralph is best known for his early work, that of making shooting decoys.

Born in Hillsboro, Illinois, in 1914, Ralph Reghi smiles as he recalls his first hunting trips there. Accompanied by his father and uncle in these early days, Ralph talks of goose hunting in the marshes of Cairo, Illinois. At the tender age of eight, waterfowling became a part of his life. When his family moved to Detroit in 1924, Ralph's yearning to hunt increased, and in the fall of 1927 he sought out Jim Kelson for advice. In this rugged man, twenty years his senior, Ralph Reghi met his inspiring force. He recalls that first meeting as being in November, remembering the deer hunting season was underway at the time.

47. Canvasback by Ralph Reghi, c. 1938.

48. Bluebill by Ralph Reghi combines balance with style.

49. Rasp marks for texture were left on Reghi canvasback, c. 1935.

50. Demure hen canvasback made by Reghi in 1938.

51. Reghi redhead drake, 1938.

During the summer of 1928, Ralph made decoys with Jim Kelson and that fall hunted with him, sneak shooting on Lake St. Clair for the first time. Ralph had realized his dream.

By the time the Depression came, the young Ralph Reghi was determined to make his living duck hunting and decoy carving. During the later years of the Depression, Ralph laughingly recalls stealing coal from Detroit Edison's Lycast Yard and selling it for 15¢ a bushel to pay for shells.

Ralph guided parties on Lake St. Clair from 1941 until 1949, except for an interrupting call to serve in Uncle Sam's Army in 1942. In 1950 Ralph gave up guiding to open his own marina in Detroit. A master craftsman and boatbuilder, he still makes his livelihood in this way.

52. Ralph Reghi bullneck canvasback made around 1938, clearly his greatest effort.

53. Canvasback hen by Ralph Reghi, 1938.

DE NAVARRE SORENSON

THE UNUSUAL DECOYS OF FERDINAND BACH (1888-1967)
by Edward T. deNavarre and Hal Sorenson

Possessing both freshness and spontaneity, the decoys of Ferdinand Bach are unlike those of any other carver. Their unique character stems partially from the unusual shape of their solid bodies—wide, somewhere between round and oval, and fairly flat. There were two reasons for this shape, Bach said: to keep them from overturning on the rough water; and to provide more "show" for high-flying birds. The unique, stylized wing carving and paint patterns were also his own.

For decoy bodies Bach preferred the large ends of old cedar telephone poles. His heads were carved from sugar pine, fastened to the body with a countersunk screw from the bottom and the hole plugged. With a draw knife, spoke shave, rasps, and a pocketknife, it took Bach only an hour to feather-carve the body of his decoy.

It is surprising that even though Bach concentrated his carving almost solely on the divers—canvasback, bluebill, redhead—which use the big water where he hunted, he used 44 different head patterns in making his last rig.

It was during a cold 1950 Michigan winter aboard a large houseboat anchored on the Clinton River that Bach, undaunted by the boathouse fire that destroyed his personal rig of 75 decoys and an 18-foot duck skiff, carved his last rig of decoys and a new skiff.

Fortunately for collectors of decoy art, a few Bach decoys survived from that 1950 rig. They are in mint condition, having been carefully cleaned and individually wrapped after each season was over.

54. Fine bill and wing carving became a feature of canvasback decoys by Ferdinand Bach.

55. Early style canvasback by Bach, perhaps his most outstanding decoy.

56. Early Bach (1920s) canvasback.

57. Bach canvasback.

58. Black duck by Bach.

59. Turned-head black, Ferdinand Bach's early style, with deep-cut wing relief.

60. Bach redhead.

61. Ferdinand Bach's early efforts produced this distinguished redhead with 1-inch bottom board.

FACTORY:

PETERSON, DODGE, AND MASON: THE COMMERCIAL MAKERS OF DETROIT
by Bernard W. Crandell

The demand for good working decoys by waterfowl hunters over the past century has been so great that three enterprising Detroiters, now famous names to collectors, responded to the needs of the market. Running ads in national sports magazines of a bygone era, they convinced hunters across the nation that their decoys would attract ducks, geese, and shorebirds.

The time frame of their ventures is interesting. George Peterson was one of the earliest decoy manufacturers in the country. Only Harvey A. Stevens of Weedsport, New York, whose products are prized by collectors, got into the market earlier, around 1866. Peterson, a carpenter and saw-maker, ran his first advertisement as a decoy maker in 1873 and continued until 1884. Jasper N. Dodge, and then William J. Mason, followed Peterson, with the Mason family staying in business the longest, around 30 years.

Peterson started his decoy business in 1873 on the second floor of a building which housed the Mellus Saw Factory. His experience as a carpenter, chairmaker, machinist, and saw-maker equipped him with excellent skills for making decoys on a duplicating lathe.

In 1875, when Peterson moved to a new location, Frank W. Lambert, a painter, joined him and in the last two years of business became his partner under the billing "Peterson and Lambert."

Peterson turned out a fine decoy, much like a Mason "Detroit" grade, only with a more pronounced breast and bill carving that included a cut for the separation of the mandibles.

One Peterson decoy has been found that still bears the remnant of a rubber stamp imprint on the bottom, although this source of identification for 100-year-old birds is poor because of the perishability of the ink. George Peterson made his decoys until 1884, when he sold the business to Jasper N. Dodge.

Although the authoritative book *American Bird Decoys* states that Dodge began making decoys at his home in 1869, the Detroit city directory does not list him as a resident until 1873, when he appeared as "clerk." He listed himself as a decoy manufacturer at his home address in 1883. By 1884 Dodge had taken over the Peterson shop.

Although Dodge used the equipment in the Peterson shop, he certainly did not utilize Peterson's patterns. Dodge's styles were quite different from Peterson's. The typical Dodge body has wide and high "shoulders" and although the bill is carved to separate it from the head, the mandibles are not separated.

Dodge made dozens, perhaps hundreds, of different body styles, primarily because he tried to copy decoy models given him by hunters who wanted their own duplicated. He advertised that he would, if provided a sample, make any kind of decoy a hunter wanted. Thus Dodge decoys do not fall into any easily identifiable grades like Mason decoys.

62. Mason challenge mallard.

63. Turned-head Mason bluebill hen (the only one known to exist).

Although Dodge advertised his products—duck, goose, snipe, and plover decoys, and duck and turkey calls—he could not attract enough business to keep going. He stopped making decoys in 1894 and went instead into oar manufacturing. From 1905 until 1908, he was president of the Detroit Canoe and Oar Works. In 1909, Jasper Dodge died at the age of eighty.

Meanwhile, Mason's decoy factory was meeting with some success. William J. Mason came to Detroit from Dublin, Ireland, with three brothers, a sister, and his parents in the early 1850s. Mason started making decoys in a shed behind his home at 49 Tuscola Street in Detroit. The exact date he launched his career commercially may never be determined, although a 1913 Mason factory advertisement ran a line stating "Established 1889." We do know that he ran a sporting goods store and that he was also an ardent sportsman, hunting ducks on the St. Clair Flats in the 1870s and 1880s.

Recently, the grandson of William J. Mason found some memorabilia in his files showing that William moved his decoy-making operation from the shed to a "factory," while still maintaining his office and salesroom at the Tuscola address. This bit of information was divulged by a piece of promotional literature, postcard size, publicizing the many species that Mason made, in particular, a pair of premier mallards. Published at the turn of the century, it was the forerunner of Mason catalogues that later pictured many species. Of the premier grade the card states: "This is positively the finest decoy made in the world. For mathematical accuracy and artistic finish, they surpass anything ever produced, flat bottom and hollow. Being flat bottomed, they ride the water in a heavy sea without the rocking motion of the round bottom decoy, and, therefore, present a perfectly natural appearance on the water. They are cut above the water line, which prevents any possibility of leakage."

The Mason factory was moved again in 1903. At this time there were approximately a dozen employees comprising the work force to operate the factory lathes, sand the birds, do the final painting, and then crate the birds for delivery to sportsmen all over the country.

Late in 1905 William J. Mason died from rheumatic fever he contracted after lying in a marsh to study ducks so that he could make his Mason decoys as realistic as possible. Herbert W. Mason, who had been doing the clerical work at the factory, took over after his father's death. Herbert moved the factory again about ten years later and continued manufacturing decoys until 1924 when he and a friend went into the paint-making business, supplying Detroit's mammoth automobile industry.

It was during Herbert W. Mason's ownership of the factory that a large mail order market for Mason decoys was built up through advertising and catalogues that illustrated the artistic qualities of the decoys. Mason was also a volume supplier to Sears Roebuck and to any sporting goods company asking to stock Mason decoys. One company was Chicago's Von Lengercke and Antoine, later acquired by Abercrombie and Fitch. Some premiers today still have the "V.L. & A. Chicago" stamped quite legibly on their bottoms.

64. Two views of canvasback believed to be Mason's earliest work—handmade, not lathemade.

65. The "St. Clair" bluebill model of Jasper Dodge of Detroit, c. 1880-94.

66. Hollow, slope-breast Canada by George Peterson of Detroit, 1873-83.

67. Mason decoy: challenge-grade lowhead bluebill hen.

Mason decoys, perhaps more than any others, are universally sought after as collectors' items. Their stylish lines, interesting heads, beautiful painting, and many poses make them irresistible art objects to many collectors. Mason "fever" continues as collectors trade and search for Masons in mint condition, especially in the rarer species. To date, two species advertised by Mason, the ruddy duck and the shoveler, have not been found. The Mason wood duck decoy is one of the rarest species: all those accounted for among collectors could easily fit into a gunny sack.

The commercial makers of Detroit have provided a rich heritage for all decoy collectors. Dodge and Mason decoys have been well known to collectors for many years, while Peterson's products have become identifiable only in the past few years. Curiously, none of the three manufacturers could have known that his talents were producing something beyond a tool to serve the sportsman. To each man, decoy manufacturing was a passing interlude in his professional life. Prosaic and mundane as decoy manufacture was in that era, it has since made a unique contribution to the world of art, and an emotional, appreciative lift to the collector who, according to the late decoy historian Joel Barber, is even more attracted to the decoys than were the ducks.

68. Mason widgeon drake, Detroit grade.

69. Mason premier widgeon pair.

70. Mason challenge mallard pair.

71. Mason premier mallard pair.

72. Challenge blue-wing teal drake by Mason.

73. Collectors debate over this blue-wing teal: Mason, Dodge, or Peterson?

74. Detroit grade green-wing teal pair by Mason.

75. Mason buffleheads, Detroit grade.

76. Mason premier sheldrake pair.

77. Mason challenge hen sheldrake.

78. Mason coot in fine original condition.

79. Mason challenge hen sheldrake.

80. A unique, early premier drake wood duck, 12½ inches long and 5¼ inches high with solid body.

81. Mason premier canvasback pair.

82. Mason canvasback.

83. Mason Back Bay model canvasbacks.

84. Dodge pintail displays pleasing profile.

85. Most unusual bird in the Jasper Dodge Co. flock is this merganser with flared head feathers.

87. Mason decoy: challenge-grade lowhead bluebill hen.

86. Mason bluebill.

88. Rare lowhead premier bluebill from Mason factory.

SWANSON

SCHROEDER

TOM SCHROEDER (1885-1976)
by Ronald S. Swanson

"The best decoys known come from the knife of Shaing Wheeler," said Joel Barber on one of his visits to Detroit in the mid-forties. That statement so irritated Tom Schroeder that he sent a group of his decoys to New York City for the 1948 National Decoy Makers' Contest. Unfortunately, most of the necks or bills were broken in shipping; but the next year Tom's entries were very carefully packed, and they won most of the ribbons. Tom had made his point.

He continued to win the major contests for several years and his influence on contemporary carvers is still obvious—attention to detail, and lifelike appearance. It might be argued that his influence on the decoy world was a negative one and that today's contemporary decoys aren't really decoys at all, but professional, mantle birds. On the other hand, it can be argued that his influences improved the marque. The fact of the matter is that his contest decoys were *working decoys* — with fifty years of carving and hunting experience to support the judges' votes. And the judges were experts, men like Wheeler, Connett, Burke, Marshall, Hunt, Mackey, and Barber.

Since the 1923 show, Shaing Wheeler had been the major influence in the contests. Winning decoys were usually carved in his Stratford style. This, of course, changed dramatically when Schroeder's work was seen in 1949.

Tom shot his first duck when he was twelve and made his first decoy shortly thereafter. He was an active sportsman throughout his life. He could shoot 99 out of 100 at skeet and, as an expert shot, he liked to hunt ducks, deer, and pheasant; one time he even got a triple on grouse. He earned a living as a cartoonist for the *Detroit News* and later made a fortune as an advertising executive. But most important of all, he was a decoy carver.

89. Tom Schroeder of Detroit carved this box-bottom redhead, c. 1937-38.

Tom Schroeder was extremly proud of his bird carvings—occasionally to the point of arrogance. He was a fiesty, self-styled perfectionist to some, while to others he was a great teacher and friend. He died in 1976 at the age of 91 in Hutzel Hospital in Detroit. The "belligerent old cuss" still had his cane by his bed to fend off the nurses.

His earliest known decoys were impressionistic in comparison to his later carefully carved and painted birds. Figure 94 shows one of his early canvasback decoys circa 1910-1920. It is very hollow with typical Flats bottom-board construction, but it stands out in many ways: it is oversized and wide with a head turn to the left creating a very contented look . . . almost puffy from overfeeding; the paint pattern is simplistic with sand added to the paint mixture to cut down on the sun's glare; the long-billed head makes a superb handle. These were minor innovations on the Flats style but all Schroeder.

Other decoys from this early rig illustrate the fact that Tom was restless and continually seeking to improve his decoys. Like most twentieth-century Detroit-area decoy makers, Tom changed over to solid decoys to avoid leakers. Few, if any, carvers made hollow decoys after World War I; perhaps wood selection was a problem. More likely, the availability of leisurely nineteenth-century time had been lost forever. On these solid decoys, Tom had begun to use a rasp to roughen the surface to further reduce the sun's glare.

His next rig indicates that he spent more time on feather detailing and he even went so far as to varnish his bird's bills to achieve a realistic gloss. By the early thirties, his decoys looked more like live ducks than any others on Lake St. Clair (see figure 93). He began to concentrate his efforts on making his decoys easier to handle and, most important of all, on what he called "hydrodynamics"—making them act like real ducks on the water.

The decoys from Tom's "1938 rig" (see figure 89) are good examples of his early concentration on hydrodynamics. The galvanized box on the bottom acts like a sea anchor. It is open at both ends; thus the water is allowed to flow through the decoy, increasing its weight and helping the bird to hold better on the water—reducing tipping and yawing. A unique two-rung ladder-shaped anchor was designed for wrapping the line. The anchor fits neatly into the box for storage, eliminating tangled decoy lines. Best of all, the decoy only had to be slipped into the water and the anchor would fall out and unwind itself for a faster setting-up time.

The "1938 rig" disappeared not long after an experiment was performed on Whitmore Lake near Ann Arbor in which Tom's rig far outpulled another rig consisting of Masons and other local decoys. About twenty of the birds from the lost rig were found and collected in 1971.

Canvasbacks, redheads, broadbills, bluebills, and two ringbills survive today. Because of the blunted tails and the box they may not be quite so appealing as some of Tom's other working decoys, but no better rig had yet been made for hunting ducks.

The drake canvasback shown in figure 91 was made in the early forties, prior to the contests. It illustrates further development in painting and carving detail—just a step away from Tom's prize-winning birds.

Comb painting replaced the rasp and Tom's subtle coloration and delicate carving is especially evident in the tail area—the most important view for an approaching duck. Innovations in hydrodynamics and handling also appear with this decoy. It is hollowed out, leaving an inch or so of the original bottom surface around the edge of the decoy. No bottom board was attached, only a deep, weighted keel which served two purposes. It was easier to carry when held upside down by the keel; and, most importantly, the exposed cavity in the bottom acted like a suction cup making the decoy ride

90. A Tom Schroeder box-bottom canvasback (c. 1937).

the waves more like its live counterpart. The galvanized tin box had been abandoned, probably because it had caused surface mars in other decoys and Tom felt more protective towards the finer painting and carving detail in his latest decoys.

The most unusual decoy Tom Schroeder ever developed is seen in figure 92. This skirt bottom canvasback decoy (which won "Best of Show" in the 1951 National Decoy Makers' Contest) is perhaps the ultimate working decoy: the sea-anchor approach to hydrodynamics seen in rough, prototype form in the box-bottom models is developed to its highest degree. The walls of the decoy are eggshell thin, and because it is so light and the cavity is proportionately so much larger, a suction-cup effect combines with the sea-anchor effect for maximum stability. The skirt is concave, providing a type of spool for wrapping the decoy's anchor line, and the opening in front is large enough for storage of the anchor.

Tom's contribution to decoy carving is important for another reason: his influence on other major carvers in the Detroit area. Over the years, Tom hunted many different areas: from Lake Erie to Saginaw Bay and from Mitchell Bay to his favorite spot to hunt cans, Fair Haven. He had been exposed to many diverse hunting situations and had seen a great many decoys in action. As a young man he had even known and hunted with Schweikart on Strawberry Island. He influenced Ferdinand Bach, as did Schweikart's decoys. Tom worked closely with Jim Kelson and Ralph Reghi in the development of their excellent hunting rigs. (Tom felt that Kelson was the greatest hunter ever on Lake St. Clair.) Tom was also very close to Ben Schmidt and "stopped by almost nightly during the forties and fifties to give him pointers."

A Tom Schroeder decoy is a rare collector's item and should be coveted regardless of the period in which it was made. His last rig, circa

91. Schroeder canvasback made around 1945.

92. Schroeder canvasback with hydrodynamic skirt bottom. (This decoy won "Best of Show" in the 1951 National Decoy Makers' Contest in New York.)

93. Schroeder bluebill, solid body.

94. Hollow Schroeder canvasback from his earliest known rig, c. 1920. Has typical stylish head.

95. Schroeder redhead with composition body.

96. Schroeder can hen with composition body on bottom board.

1955, was composed of the composite decoys which were light and easy to make. They are important because of their terminal position in the spectrum of his development (see figure 97).

Schroeder hunting decoys have been extremely difficult to collect for two reasons: first of all, he never carved professionally and only kept a working rig of about fifty birds, some of which were replaced from time to time as they were lost or became, in his opinion, obsolete. Secondly, as a proud artist and skilled craftsman full of self-confidence and strong opinions, he tried to keep almost every decoy he ever made. He gave away only a few decoys: some to Joel Barber, which ended up in the Shelbourne Museum in Vermont, some to proteges or friends, and very few to collectors.

97. Canvasback drake low and highhead models with composition bodies by Schroeder in 1955.

SCHMIDT

BEN SCHMIDT (1884-1968)
by William J. Mackey, Jr.

Ben Schmidt made a virile, husky, working decoy; the kind a knowing hunter felt confident to be shooting over.

I was shown pictures of Ben's decoys for years before I hefted one. What a difference. Two dimensional pictures simply do not do justice to his decoys. Only in the wood does one get the appeal of Schmidt's decoys. They are husky and physically adequate for their appointed task. Oversized, yes, but not in an exaggerated sense; heavy, yes, but with a balanced keel and weight that gives each bird the fine visibility which is the most important phase of the game.

Fault Ben, if you wish, on fussy little details, but the overall effectiveness of his skill gave duck hunters just about the closest thing to the all-American working decoy. Even his sketchy and seemingly haphazard carving and checking has its charm. I can't believe that his decoys would have been as effective without the added checks and grooves. The time he spent with these fussy details staggers the imagination. These extra touches might seem superfluous to some, but without them much of the charm of a Ben Schmidt decoy would be lost. His work has earned a place in the annals of American folk art.

98. Ben Schmidt mallard hen.

99. Early pintail pair by Ben Schmidt.

100. Ben Schmidt mallard pair.

101. Mallards by Ben Schmidt.

102. The favorite of many Detroit duck hunters was the Ben Schmidt mallard.

103. Rare Ben Schmidt blue goose has appealing head.

104. Canada goose by Ben Schmidt.

105. Variation in blue goose style by Ben Schmidt.

106. Pintail drake working decoy, typical of the fine style of Ben Schmidt.

Though not as well known as his brother Ben, Frank Schmidt was a skillful carver in his own right. Ben's decoys have an unmistakable finesse, while Frank's are bolder with heavier lines. Illustrated here is work typical of the Schmidts in goose, bluebill, and black duck decoys, placed side by side for comparison. Shown elsewhere in this volume (see figure 12) is a very rare working ruddy duck decoy by Frank Schmidt.

107. Canada Goose by Frank Schmidt

108. Bluebill hen by Ben Schmidt.

109. Bluebill decoy by Frank Schmidt.

110. Ben Schmidt black duck, a collector's favorite.

111. Ben Schmidt Canada goose.

112. Frank Schmidt black duck has good proportions.

CLUB CARVERS
by Bernard W. Crandell

The private duck hunting clubs of the St. Clair Flats, the Detroit River, and western Lake Erie have been prime retail markets for the really superior decoy carvers from the 1870s on up to the present. Club members have traditionally wanted not only the best hunting that was obtainable but also the very best quality in their equipment. And they have been able to afford it.

They belonged, around Lake St. Clair, to such famous clubs as the Lake St. Clair Fishing and Shooting Club (now the Old Club), Mud Creek, St. Anne's, Big Pointe, St. Luke's, Dover, Balmoral, Bradley's, and the St. Clair Flats Shooting Company, Ltd., also known as the Canada Club and the Toronto Club. Down river on the Michigan side and along western Lake Erie were the Erie Shooting Club, Monroe Marsh Club, and the Pointe Mouillee Shooting Club, to mention only some of the major acreages, although the latter two have long since passed into history. Along the marshes across the Detroit River in Canada were many more clubs, most of them American-owned. Many of the

CLUB CARVERS

finest decoys now reposing on collectors' shelves have come from these sources.

Oldest of all the clubs is the appropriately-named Old Club on Harsens Island in the St. Clair Flats. Although it is now a boat club, it was founded by a group of Detroiters in 1872 as the Lake St. Clair Fishing and Shooting Club. They put up the first clubhouse on the Flats and, of more interest to collectors, had a famous carver among their members. On the 1888 membership list of the club there appears "W.J. Mason," the founder of Mason's Decoy Factory of Detroit. William Mason, then a sporting goods store owner and an ardent sportsman, used his own handmade decoys until 1896, when he began manufacturing decoys with lathes. Some of his handmades still are around today, one being a canvasback pictured in the Shelbourne Museum catalogue.

Members of the Pointe Mouillee Shooting Club were attracted to the fine carpentry and craftsmanship of one of their punters, Nate Quillen, who made duck boats and decoys in the last quarter of the 1800s with such skill that club members didn't have to look further for this important equipment. Quillen sold his solid body decoys — the ones that had a knot in the wood precluding hollowing the body — to members for only 50 cents each. The hollow gems that came out of his workshop went for $1, a fair price in those days when decoys were strictly for utility, but a striking contrast to their value today to collectors willing to pay several hundred times that amount for a Quillen to grace their shelves. Quillen decoys made their way into the collectors' world haphazardly after the club

113. Canvasback stamped Thos. Chambers.

114. Hollow black, unknown origin, from St. Clair Flats Shooting Co.

115. Chambers black duck, c. 1915.

folded, just as most fine club decoys do . . . a few sold by members to other hunters, a few given away to friends, and a few that drifted away in a storm to be picked up and placed in rigs far distant from home.

Rarely, if ever, has the entire group of decoys used at a club over the past 100 years gone intact to collectors. But this unusual event occurred in 1975, when approximately 900 duck and goose decoys of the 101-year-old St. Clair Flats Shooting Company, which was facing lease renewal problems with the Walpole Island Indian band, were sold by the club to collectors. This decoy bonanza, which has been shared with collectors countrywide, comprised the best work of Tom Chambers, manager of the club from 1900 to 1943, George Warin, one of the club's founders in 1874, and John R. Wells, the famed "JRW MAKER." All of these makers, incidentally, were from Toronto. In addition, there were several Quillen decoys, brought in by a member, Dr. Harry N. Torrey, after the demise of the Pointe Mouillee Club, his previous association. There were also a number of Masons, Dodges, and Petersons, the latter being the first known examples of goose decoys by the earliest of the Detroit commercial makers. The goose decoys, all in original paint and nearly all of them hollow, represented the artistic effort of at lease nine different makers. In addition to those made by George Peterson, there were several by Tom Chambers, George and James Warin, John Reeves, manager of the club for a few years in the late 1880s, Jasper Dodge, David Ward, one of the club's founders, and some "unknowns." David Ward's creations only rarely have the "D WARD" burned on the bottom and their heads are remarkably like Warin's; an

116. Classic canvasback by Tom Chambers (c. 1915).

117. Bluebill hen, round-head style, by Chambers.

118. Solid body ringbill by George Warin.

119. Redhead by Warin, from St. Clair Flats Co., c. 1878.

120. Pintail, maker unknown, Port Rowan, Ontario.

understandable resemblace since he was George Warin's great personal friend and shooting buddy. At one time, Ward's goose decoys were owned by Tom Chambers as Tom burned his "THOS. CHAMBERS" on the bottom. Chambers, however, was careful not to add his "MAKER" stamp.

In the early years the marsh ducks primarily were blacks; thus a great number of black duck decoys, by many makers and of many poses and styles, were a part of the St. Clair Flats Shooting Company group. Chambers, Warin, and Wells all made handsome lowheads, while Chambers and Wells also made some outstanding highheads. Among the "unknown" black lowheads there also are some real works of art — hollow with thin bottom boards and graceful proportions. Surprisingly, only a relatively few mallards by Chambers, Warin, and unknown

121. Lowhead black duck by Tom Chambers.

makers were in the flock. Certainly the largest of the mallards were half a dozen oversize balsas made by Ralph Coykendall, an author on decoy making. Ringbills apparently were popular targets as George Warin made a number of decoys to attract this species. Pintail decoys were a scarce item, but the few that Chambers and Warin made were masterpieces, one of the latter being in the Shelbourne Museum catalogue attributed to George "Warren." In the diver category, redheads, canvasbacks, and bluebills were hunted by the club members. But, judging from the fine condition of the decoys of these species, many of which are 100 years old, they must not have hunted them very much.

The Chambers canvasbacks and redheads were practically all in original paint and from good to mint condition. Chambers made cans with both long and short bodies, and in both his early roundhead and later flathead styles. He also made redheads in both the long and short body versions, and with at least three different head styles. Only a few bluebills came off the Chambers bench. There is something unforgettable about the Chambers decoy profiles, especially the noble canvasbacks which have excellent combing. Most Chambers decoys have the typical "Flats" hollow body with

122. Tom Chambers canvasback.

bottom board. Only a few of his blocks had solid bodies.

George and James Warin, the Toronto boat builders, made a number of redheads and bluebills, both solid and hollow bodies, some marked "G & J Warin Builders Toronto" for George's and other members' use at the club. Since George hunted on the "Flats" before the company was founded, many of his decoys are believed to be around 110 years old. The Warins made very few canvasbacks. They had several body and head styles for their bluebills and redheads and their painting had many fine examples of combing and feathering.

Diver duck decoys made for club members by John Wells were cans and redheads, among the finest of all "Flats" style blocks. One of the club members who was impressed with the JRW style, and burned his name on the thin bottom boards of many of Well's finest decoys, was Truman H. Newberry (membership, 1900-1914) of Grosse Pointe, Michigan, a former U.S. Senator and Secretary of the Navy in Theodore Roosevelt's cabinet.

Perhaps the most unusual of all the decoys of the St. Clair Flats Shooting Company were the swans, seven of which are believed to exist. They originally were used at the turn of the century by a hunter in the vicinity of Mitchell Bay of Lake St. Clair. The late Charles Bolton, of nearby Wallaceburg, Ontario, came across them when taking electrical wiring out of the owner's cottage, and found they were for sale. Bolton purchased two, while five went to the

123. Phineas Reeves pintail (c. 1866) shows fine plumage by the former decorative painter from Port Rowan, Ontario.

club. They were used there by members primarily in the spring of the year when swans were migrating northward. The present owner of two of the swans is William R. Miller, regional enforcement supervisor for the Canadian Wildlife Service, who relates:

"The late Cliff Roy, manager of the club, presented one such decoy to me in 1962 and later the same year I obtained one from the widow of Charles Bolton, who had had two of them in his possession for 40 years. Roy told me that three of the club's swans had migrated with a member to Long Island, and two remained at the club.

"Upon acquisition of my first swan I could hardly wait to get back to the motel at which time I filled the bathtub and proved my initial surmise that there was no way the decoy could float in an upright position unless a very heavy counterweight of some type was added. This in itself belies the fact these decoys are hollow, I suspect even to a portion of the neck.

"I finally solved the mystery in that the swan at the club at that time still had attached a 3-3/4 x 3-3/4 inch castplate with a flange 1-1/4 inch in diameter extending downward about 3/4 inch. Obviously these birds were set on a cut stick that was pushed down into the marsh bottom. I feel certain that the decoy flotation was such that the bird could not have had more than 2 inches of water depth extending up the side of the decoy. The method of placement would allow the decoy to pivot in the wind and I suspect would greatly enhance a goose rig, especially if the swans were set along the shoreline and apart from the geese. This does clarify my puzzlement as to how the birds were set out."

The era of private duck hunting clubs in the St. Clair Flats is on the decline. There have been no major clubs on the U.S. side for many years, while some on the Ontario side are disappearing under the combined pressure of the Walpole Island Indian band and the Canadian government. The Indian band, wanting more marshland for its own uses, is outpricing even the wealthier groups of sportsmen with costlier lease demands. The Canadian government, wanting more marsh for sanctuary and study purposes, already has purchased the old Dover club and is looking for other acreage.

What this means to the collector is that these excellent repositories of choice decoy art may only a little longer have such custodianship for the collector of the future.

124. Tom Chambers, St. Clair Flats Shooting Company, 1900-40, black duck.

125. Pintail drake decoy.

99

126. Redhead drake by Thomas Chambers.

127. Pintail exhibits the best of Chambers.

128. Drake pintail with delicate combing is product of "G & J WARIN BUILDERS TORONTO," by George Warin in 1876.

129. Thomas S. Dalton, a Hamilton, Ontario, boat builder, c. 1885, made this pair of redheads.

130. Hollow canvasback with fine scratch painting believed to be the work of John R. Wells, St. Clair Flats Shooting Co.

131. Compact hollow redhead, 13 inches from bill to tail, believed to be a JRW, from St. Clair Flats Shooting Co.

12
OTHER CARVERS

132. Alert whistler came from the knife of Otto Misch of the Saginaw Bay area, c. 1935.

133. Fine old Misch canvasback.

STRUBING

134. Walter Strubing of Marine City made this hollow, oversized, classic can.

135. Walter Strubing whistler, a seaworthy diver used on the St. Clair River.

KELLIE

136. Canvasback pair by Ed "One Arm" Kellie of Monroe.

137. Kellie redhead.

138. Kellie two-thirds size bluebill.

139. Ed Kellie of Monroe made this very presentable two-thirds size bluebill hen.

109

13 OTHER DECOYS

140. Classic goose by Chambers.

141. George Warin made this goose decoy in 1876.

142. Hollow Canada goose, maker unknown, used at the St. Clair Flats Shooting Co. in late 1800s.

GOOSE DECOYS

143. A Tom Chambers hollow Canada goose.

144. David Ward, Toronto pawnbroker and shooting partner of George Warin, made this hollow goose for use at his club, the St. Clair Flats Shooting Co., in 1876.

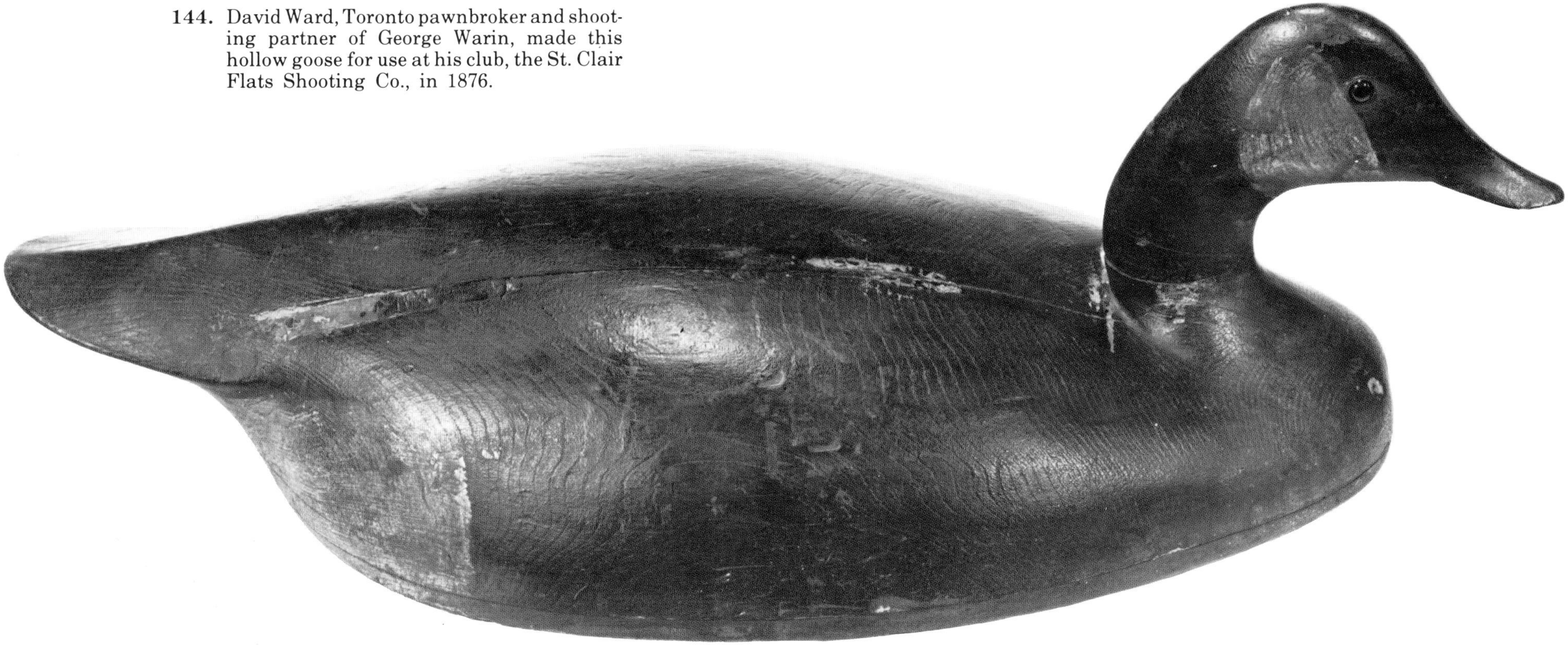

145. John Reeves of Port Rowan, Ontario, made this stylish goose when he managed the St. Clair Flats Shooting Co. from 1882 to 1896.

HERON & SNIPE

146. Charlie Pozzini heron—one of a kind.

147. A Canada Club Wilson's snipe, George Hendrie maker.

148. Turned-head canvasback by Ted Vandenboesch of Mt. Clemens, in a graceful pose.

149. Hollow canvasback drake of Flats origin. Unknown vintage and maker.

150. David Ward canvasback from the 1860s.

151. Floyd Crooks of Tom Run made this canvasback with unusual bill delineation.

152. Gigantic canvasback by John Zachmann of Detroit with Mason canvasback for size comparison.

153. Canvasback pair by G. DeCoe from Marine City area.

154. Three unusual canvasbacks, makers unknown.

155. Unusual hollow canvasback hen.

156. Michigan canvasback by an unknown maker.

157. Canvasback drake by Alexander "Yock" Meldrum of Fair Haven on Lake St. Clair (c. 1912).

158. Canvasback decoy, maker unknown.

159. Canvasback by unknown maker displays graceful silhouette.

160. Sampier canvasback (c. 1890).

161. Canvasback decoy, maker unknown.

BLACK DUCKS & MALLARDS

162. Two views of black duck in alert attitude by Thomas Steiner.

163. Mallard pair by Frank Cummings of Harsens Island, Lake St. Clair.

164. Three black duck decoys by John Finch.

165. Turned-head black duck by Frank Cummings.

166. Joe Meyer of Mitchells Bay made this handsome black duck out of a 20-inch pine log.

168. Ed Lamerand of Flat Rock was meticulous in feathering and wing carving, evident in these decoys.

167. Unique tip-up black duck decoy: as it would be seen sitting on the water (above) and in feeding attitude (below). Maker unknown.

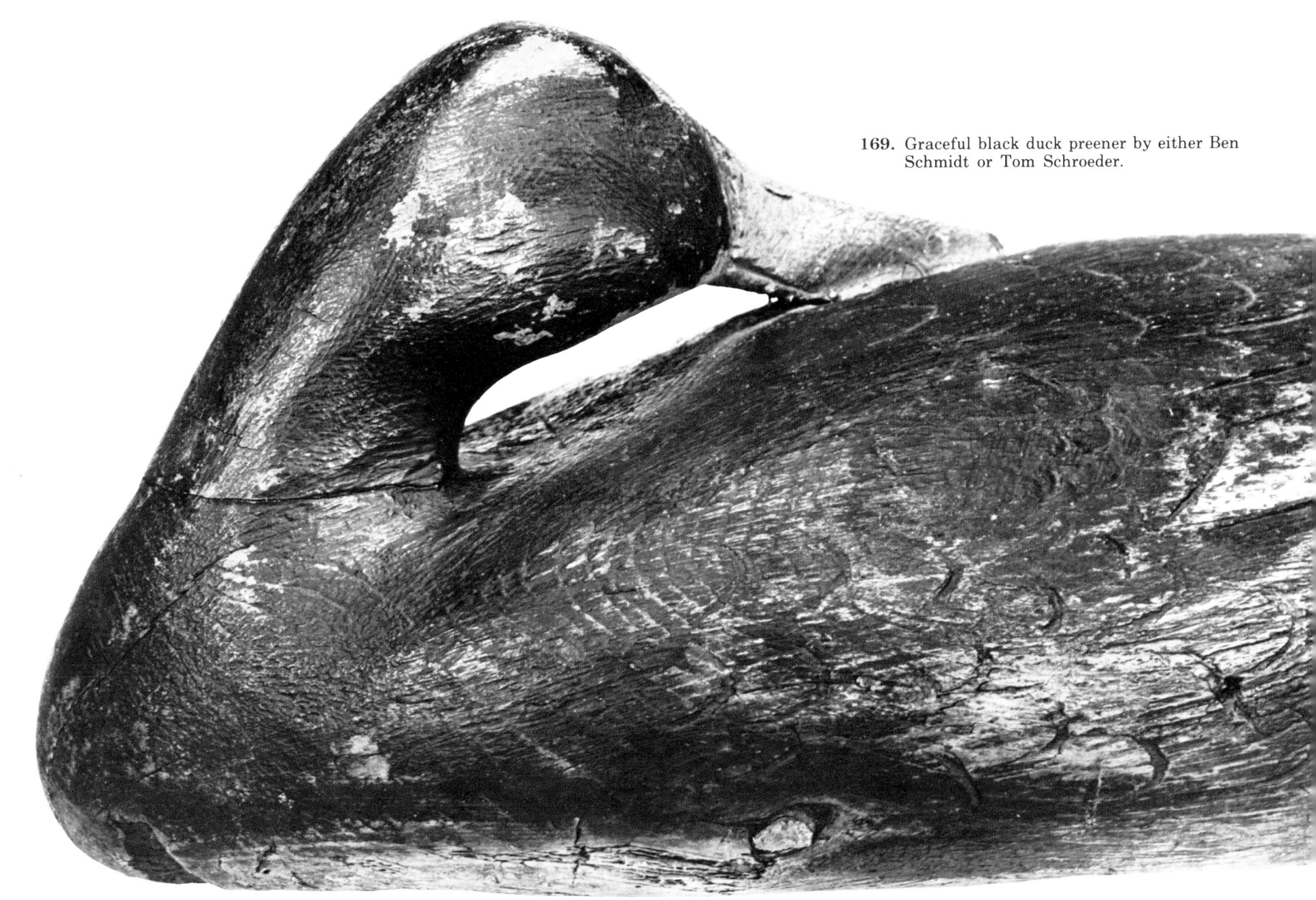

169. Graceful black duck preener by either Ben Schmidt or Tom Schroeder.

170. Black, made collectively by Bernard, Henry, and William Christie, bachelor brothers who moved from Detroit to Au Gres in 1918.

171. Graceful black by John Finch of Port Huron.

172. Mallard by George Hendrie.

173. Black with good feathering and wing carving, and a great head, by Leo Pashpatel of Harsens Island, c. 1950.

174. Zeke McDonald of MacDonald's Island in the St. Clair Flats carved this bird, c. 1910.

175. William Finkel black duck.

WHISTLERS

176. Lake Erie drake whistler by an unknown maker.

177. Hollow whistler by Russ Wilkinson of Leamington, Ontario, exhibits the usual startling golden-eye look.

178. Whistler by Danny Scriven, c. 1925, is example of lower Detroit River bobtail.

179. High-domed whistler decoy was found on Lake Erie around 1900.

180. Handsome whistler from St. Clair Flats, maker unknown.

BUFFLEHEADS

181. Fine pair of buffleheads, makers unknown.

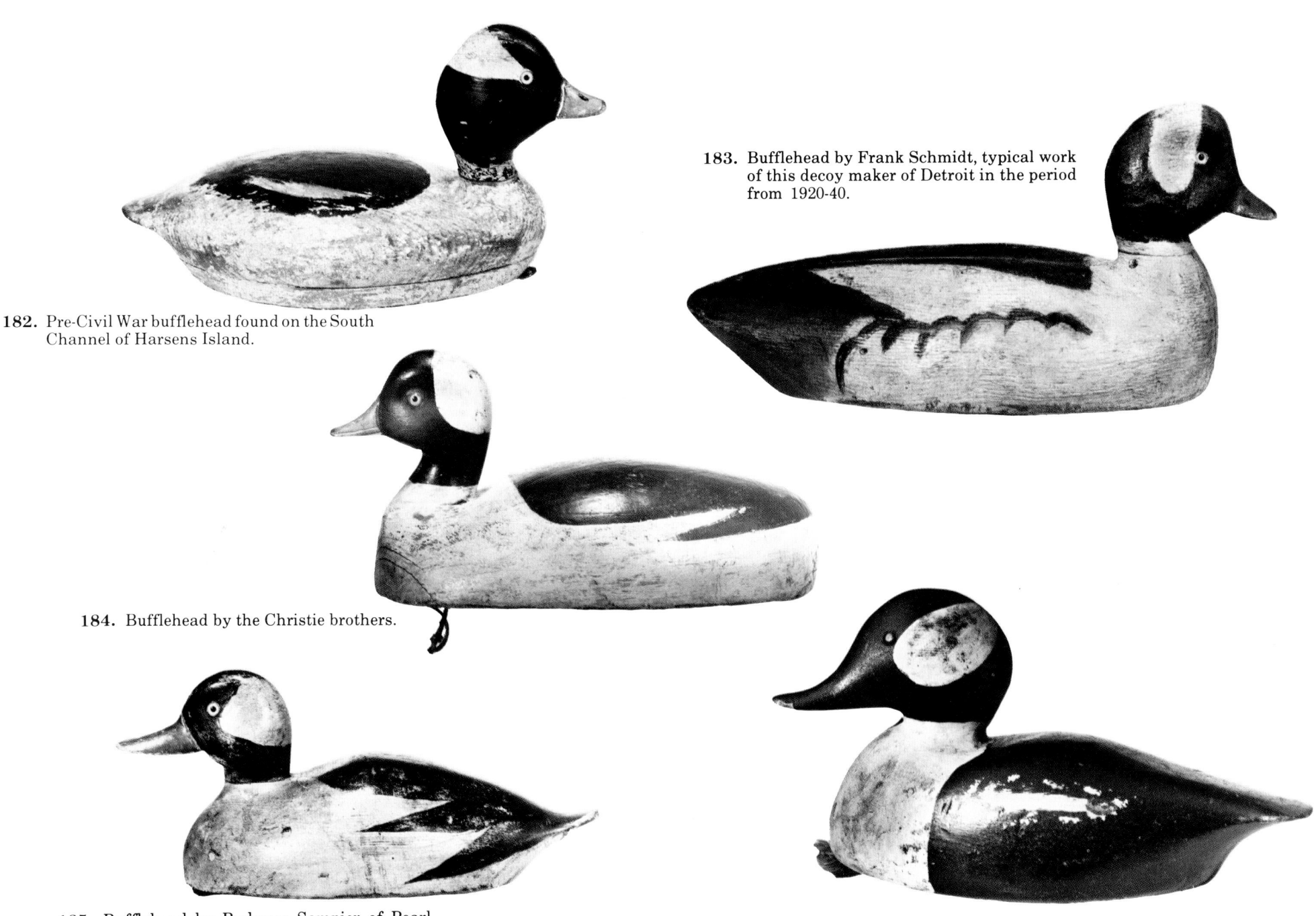

182. Pre-Civil War bufflehead found on the South Channel of Harsens Island.

183. Bufflehead by Frank Schmidt, typical work of this decoy maker of Detroit in the period from 1920-40.

184. Bufflehead by the Christie brothers.

185. Bufflehead by Budgeon Sampier of Pearl Beach.

186. Interesting bufflehead decoy. Maker unknown.

187. Two unusual Michigan buffleheads by unknown makers.

LOWHEADS

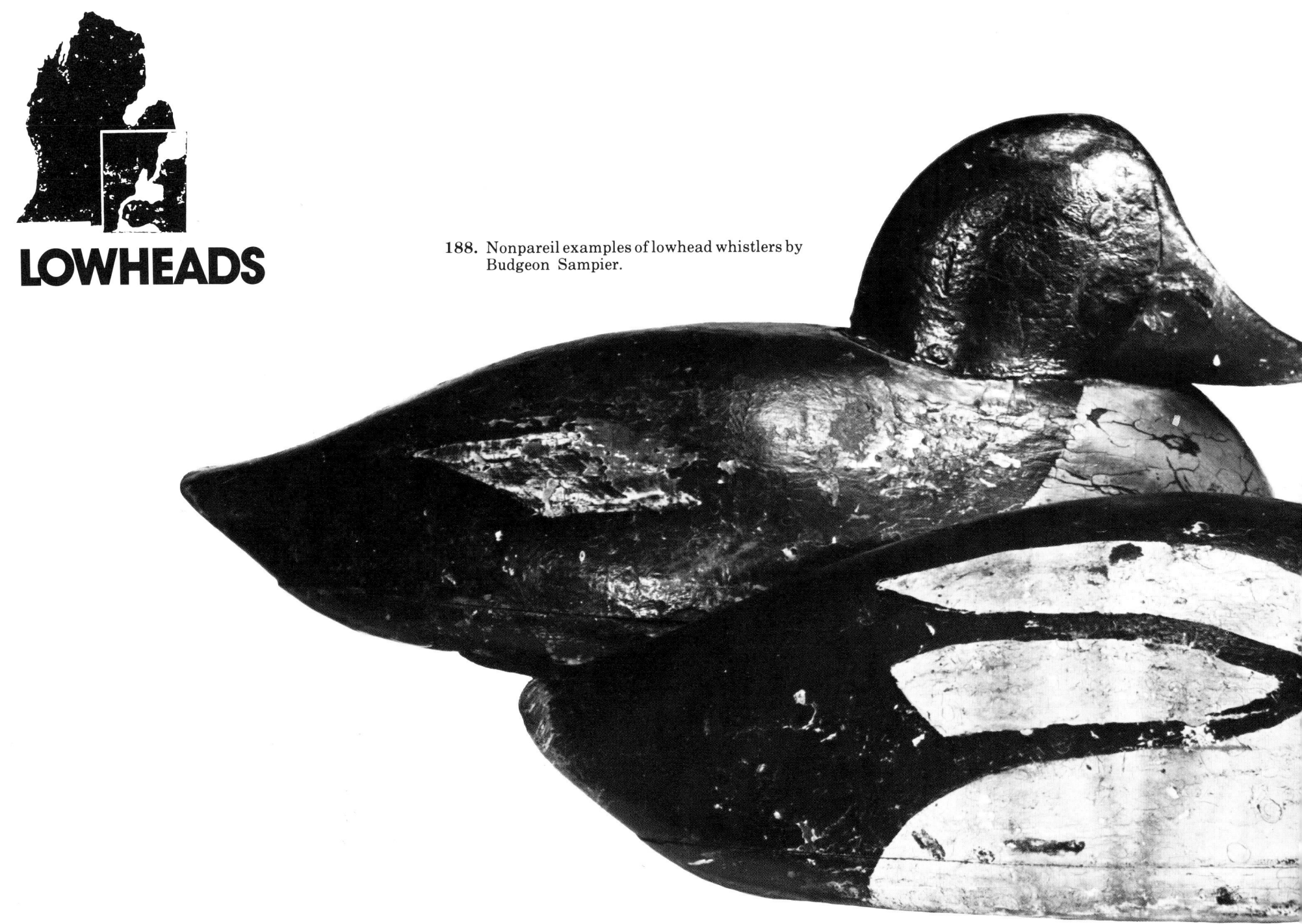

188. Nonpareil examples of lowhead whistlers by Budgeon Sampier.

189. Lowhead whistler, maker unknown, of type found on Harsens Island and Long Point Bay.

190. Three uncommon examples of the lowhead decoy style, all by unknown makers.

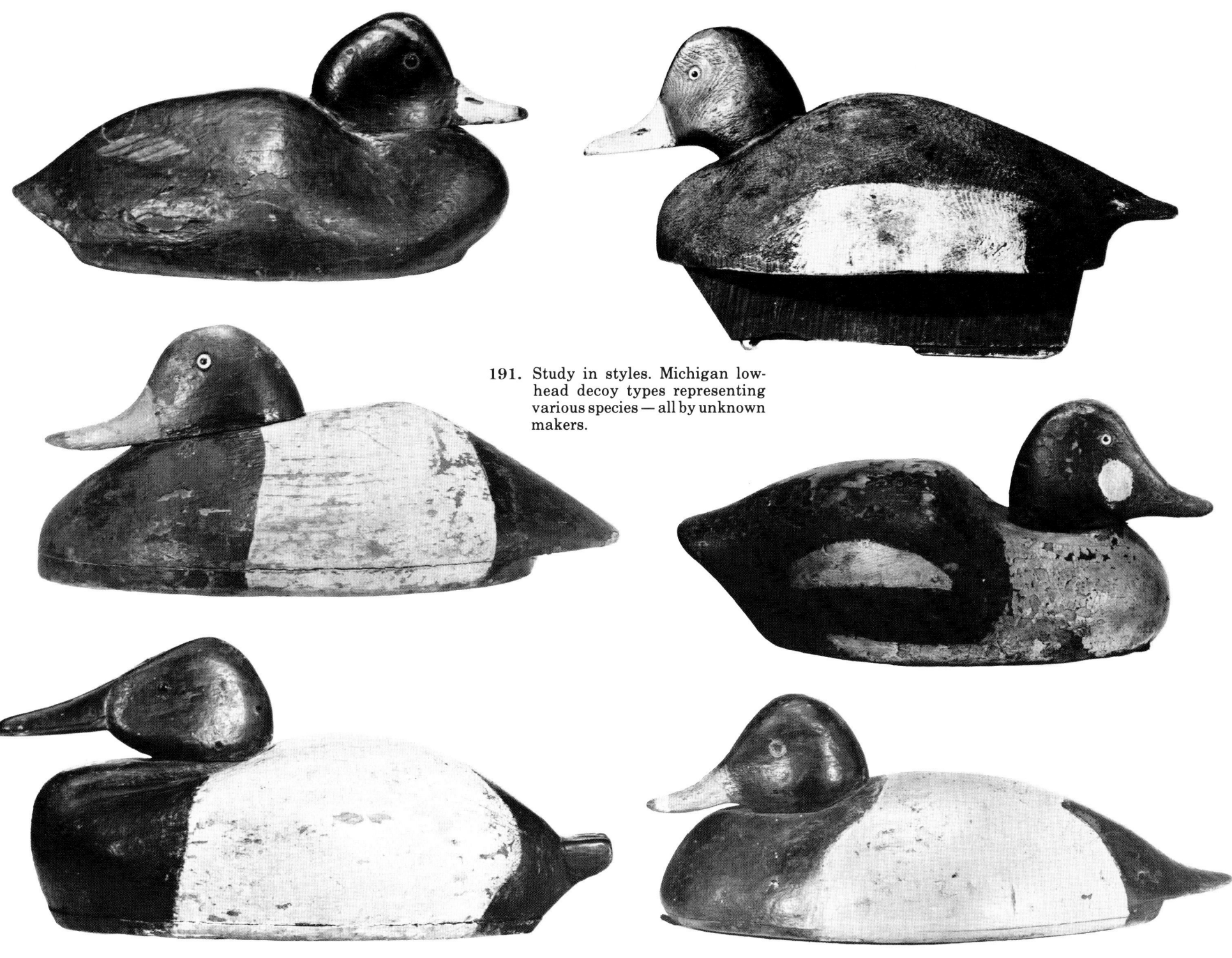

191. Study in styles. Michigan low-head decoy types representing various species — all by unknown makers.

192. Lowhead decoys: a John Schweikart canvasback and a C. C. Smith redhead.

LONGNECKS

193. High-head cans by Scott Peters.

194. A longneck canvasback by an unknown maker.

195. High-head, humped-back, hollow canvasback carved by Scott Peters, c. 1925.

145

196. Redhead of unknown origin.

197. "St. Clair Flats Longneck" redhead.

198. Tobin Meldrum canvasback high head, c. 1900.

199. Tobin Meldrum of Pearl Beach, a tiny community on the north shore of Lake St. Clair, produced this hollow, flat bottomed, high-head redhead, c. 1900.

200. Redhead of William Finkel displays charming pose.

REDHEADS

201. Distinctive head styling was a McDonald feature, expecially on his redheads.

202. C.C. Smith redhead.

203. Redhead sleeper, maker unknown.

204. Redhead by boat builder John Morris of Hamilton, Ontario, c. 1900.

205. Redhead drake from the "Flats Club" by an unknown maker.

MERGANSERS

206. Hooded merganser, maker unknown, Lake St. Clair.

207. American merganser, by the Christie brothers, is only decoy of this species known to have been made in Michigan.

208. Extremely rare hooded merganser decoy by Charles Mailloux, Lighthouse Cove, Ontario.

209. Many Purdo canvasback heads like these three fine examples are found on Ben Schmidt cans. Nick sold them to Ben in the 1950s.

210. Redhead with excellent head carving by Nick Purdo.

211. Lowhead canvasback, maker unknown.

212. Canvasback pair by Alfred Dreschel.

213. Unusual pairs of bluewing teal by Finch.

TEAL

214. Unique teal pair believed to have been made by George Hendrie, longtime member of the St. Clair Flats Shooting Co.

BLUEBILLS & RINGBILLS

215. Ringbill decoys. Maker: Doc Baumgartner.

216. Bluebill decoys by Alfred Dreschel.

217. Hollow bluebill with unusual body conformation.

INDEX

References to illustrations are printed in italic.
References to page numbers are printed in roman.

Aluminum wing tips (Schweikart), *37, 38,* 30-31
Au Gres, Christie brothers' black duck and, *170*

Bach, Ferdinand, 25
    biographical sketch of, 42
    black duck by *58, 59*
    canvasback decoys by, *54, 55, 56, 57*
    redhead by, *61*
    Schroeder and, 76
Back Bay, canvasback by Mason factory and, *83*
Balsa decoys, 95
    bluewing teal by Finch, *213*
    canvasback pair by Dreschel, *212*
    by Kelson, *43, 46*
    by Kelson and Reghi, 33-34
    lowhead canvasback (maker unknown), *211*
    Purdo's canvasback heads on Ben Schmidt's decoys, *209*
    redhead decoy by Purdo, *210*
Barber, Joel, 56, 72
    Quillen's lowheads and, 14
    Schroeder's decoys and, 79
Barbour, William T., 17
Barnegat, 23
Baumgartner, Doc, ringbill by, *215*
Belle Isle, 30
Bill carving, Unger and, 23
Black duck, 94
    by Bach, *58*
    by Chambers, *115, 124*
        lowhead, *121*
    by Christie brothers, *170*
    by Cummings, *165*
    by Finch, *164, 171*
    by Finkel, *175*
    by Lamerand, *168*
    by McDonald, *174*
    by Meyer, *166*
    by Pashpatel, *173*
    from St. Clair Flats Shooting Co. (makers unknown), *114*
    by Schmidt (Ben and Frank), *110, 111, 112, 169*
    by Schroeder, *169*
    by Steiner, *162*
    tip-up (maker unknown), *167*
    by Unger, 23, *34*
Bluebill
    by Bach, 42
    boat-body (Quillen), *28, 29*
    by Dodge factory, *65*
    by Dreschel, *216*
    hollow (maker unknown), *217*
    by Kellie (two-thirds size), *138, 139*
    Kelson's balsa, *43*
    by Mason factory, *63, 67, 86, 87, 88*
    by Reghi, *46, 48*
    round-head hen (Chambers), *117*
    by Schmidt (Ben), Plates 14-15, *108*
    by Schmidt (Frank), *107, 109*
    by Schroeder, Plates 4-5, *74*
    by Schweikart, 25
    solid body (Schroeder), *93*
Blue goose. *See* Goose, blue
Bolton, Charles, 96, 97
Bottom boards
    on Bach's redhead, *61*
    on Schroeder's decoys, 75
        canvasback hen of, *96*
Box-bottom decoys
    canvasback by Schroeder, *90*
    redhead by Schroeder, *89*
Broadbills (Schroeder), *74*
Bufflehead
    by Christie brothers, *184*
    hollow drake (Malinski), *4*
    Mason factory, 75
    pair of (maker unknown), *181*
    pre-Civil War (Harsen's Island, maker unknown), *182*
    pre-Civil War (lowhead, maker unknown), *5*
    by Sampier, *185*
    by Schmidt, (Frank), *183*
    by unknown makers, *5, 181, 186, 187*
Bullneck style decoy canvasback
    Mt. Clemens and, 25
    by Reghi, *16, 52*
    by Schweikart, *37*

Cairo, Illinois, 36
Canada Club, 88
    goose decoys of, Plates 12-13
    Hendrie's Wilson's snipe and, *147*
Canada goose. *See* Goose, Canada
Cans. *See* Canvasback
Canvasback, Plate *16*
    analysis of Michigan decoys and, 3-13
    by Bach, 42, *54, 55, 56, 57*
    balsa pair (Dreschel), *212*
    bobtailed (maker unknown), *20*
    bobtailed (Wallach), *21*
    bullneck (Reghi), *14, 16, 52*
    bullneck (Schweikart), *27, 37, 38*
    bullneck style (Mt. Clemens), *25*
    by Chambers, *23, 24, 94, 95-96, 116, 122*
    by DeCoe, *153*
    drake (Alexander Meldrum), *157*
    high-head hollow (Peters), *195*
    high-head (Peters), *193*
    high-head (Tobin Meldrum), *198, 199*
    hollow drake (McDonald), *25*
    hollow (St. Clair Flats, maker unknown), *149*
    by Kellie, *136*
    by Kelson, *32*
        balsa, *43*
    lowhead balsa (maker unknown), *211*
    lowhead (Schweikart), *26, 39, 192*
    lowhead (Smith Co.), *8*

218. Buffleheads by Otto Misch (foreground) and Stanley Alexander.

Mason factory, Plates 6-7, *64, 81, 82, 83, 152*
by Misch, *133*
Purdo's heads on Ben Schmidt's, *209*
by Reghi, Plate 8, *47, 49, 50, 53,*
    bullneck, *14, 16, 52*
reptilian aspect of head ("snaky-head"), 7-12
St. Clair Flats (maker unknown), *9*
by Sampier, *160*
by Schmidt (Ben), Plates 14-15, *15*
    Purdo's balsa heads on, *209*
by Schroeder, Plates 4-5, *74, 90, 91, 92, 94,*
    drake, *97*
    hen, *96*
by Schweikart, Plates 2-3, *25, 26, 27, 29, 38, 40*
    bullneck (aluminum wing tip), *27, 37*
    lowhead, *26, 39, 192*
    tin-wing, *13*
sleeper (St. Anne's Club), *27*
sleeper (Zachmann), *26*
by Strubing, *18, 19, 134*
turned-head (Vandenboesch), *148*
by Unger, *33, 34*
    analysis of, 21-23
by unknown maker, *9, 17, 20, 149, 154, 155, 156, 158, 159, 161, 194*
by Ward (David), *150*
by Warin, *22*
by Wells, *130, 131*
by Zachmann
    gigantic sized, *152*
    sleeper, *26*

Carnaghi, Len, 36
Carvers. *See names of specifc individuals*
Carving techniques
    aesthetic principles and, 2
    Bach's, 42
    Kelson and Reghi and, 33-34
    Lamerand's meticulous, *168*
    Michigan decoys and, xvi
    Pashpatel's, *173*
    Quillen's (described by Foote), 16-17
    schools of carving and, 25
    Zachmann's sleeper canvasback and, 12

Catana, Jerry, 32
C.C. Smith Co.
    lowhead canvasback, *8*
    lowhead redhead, *192*
    redhead, *202*
Chambers, Tom, xxiii, 31
    black duck by, *115, 124*
        lowhead, *121*
    bluebill by, *117*
    canvasback by, *23, 24, 113, 116, 122*
        analysis of, 12
    decoys by, Plate 16
    goose by, *140*
    hollow Canada goose by, *143*
    pintail by, *127*
    redhead drake by, *126*
    St. Clair Flats Shooting Co. and, 91, 94, 95-96
    wood duck by, Plate 16
Chesapeake Bay region, 23
Christie brothers (Bernard, Henry, and William)
    black duck by, *170*
    bufflehead by, *184*
    merganser by, *207*
Clinton River, Kelson and, *44*
Cobb, Nathan, 24
Cobb's Island, Unger's decoys and, 23
Collectibles (decoys as), 5-16, 12
    factory made decoys as, 56
Combing (painting technique). *See also* Painting
    Chamber's decoys and, *23*
    on drake pintail by Warin, *128*
    Schroeder's decoys and, 75
Common snipe. *See* Wilson's snipe
Composite decoys (Schroeder), 79
Composition body (Schroeder), *96, 97*
Coot
    Mason factory, Plates 6-7, *78*
    by Schweikart, *25, 42*
Coykendall, Ralph, 95
Crandell, Bernard W., 14, 88
Crooks, Floyd, canvasback by, *151*
Crowell, Elmer, 27
Cummings, Frank
    mallard pair by, *163*
    turned-head black duck by, *165*

Dalton, Thomas S., redhead pair by, *129*
DeCoc, G., canvasbacks by, *153*
Decoy poses. *See names of specific decoy styles, e.g.* Sleeper style decoy, *etc.*
Decoys. *See* Drake decoys; Gunning decoys; Hen decoys; Hollow decoys; Solid decoys; *names of specific carvers; names of specific type of decoy, e.g.* Black duck, Canvasback, Merganser, *etc.; specfic type of decoy pose, e.g.,* Feeding style decoy, *etc.*
Decoys as collectibles, 5-6, 12
    factory made decoys as, 56
Delaware River, 23
deNavarre, Edward T., 42
Detroit
    bufflehead by Frank Schmidt and, *183*
    Schweikart family and, 30

Detroit River (lower), whistler (bobtail) by Scriven and, *178*
Diver duck
    Bach's decoys and, 42

219. Early widgeon and canvasback by Ben Schmidt.

Unger's hollow heads and, 23
Unger's tail differences and, *34*
Dodge factory, 91
    analysis of, 48-51, 56
    bluewing teal, *73*
    instability of decoys and, 21
    merganser, *85*
    pintail, *84*
    "St. Clair" bluebill, *65*
Dodge, Jasper, 48, 49, 91
Drake decoy. *See also* Hen decoy
    bluewing teal (Mason factory), *72*
    canvasback (Alexander Meldrum), *157*
    canvasback (Schroeder), *74*
    greenwing teal (Schmidt), Plates 14-15
    high and lowhead canvasback (Schroeder), *97*
    hollow bufflehead (Malinski), *4*
    hollow canvasback (McDonald), *25*
    Lake Erie whistler (maker unknown), *176*
    mallard (Kelson), *44*
    mallard (Schroeder), Plates 4-5
    pintail (Mason factory), Plates 6-7
    pintail (Schmidt), Plates 14-15, *106*
    pintail (Warin), *128*
    redhead drake (Chambers), *126*
    redhead ("Flats Club," maker unknown), *205*
    redhead (Quillen), *31*
    redhead (Reghi), *51*
    whistler (Schmidt), *10*
    whistler (Schweikart), *36*
    widgeon (Mason factory), *68*
    widgeon (Quillen), *31*
    wood duck (solid, Mason factory), *80*
Dreschel, Alfred
    balsa canvasback pair by, *212*
    bluebill by, *216*
Duck hunting boats, Quillen and, 14, 17-18

220. Uncommon hollow bufflehead from St. Clair Flats area.

Dudley, Lem, 24
Dusky duck. *See* Black duck

"Egg shell" decoys, 23
Ellison, Phyllis, xiv, xvi
Erie Shooting Club, 88

Factory decoys. *See* Dodge factory; Mason factory; Peterson factory
Fair Haven (Lake St. Clair), Meldrum's canvasback drake and, 157
Feeding style decoy, widgeon, *1*
Finch, John
    balsa bluewing teal by, *213*
    black ducks by, *164, 171*
Finkel, William
    black duck by, *175*
    high-head redhead by, *200*
Flat-bottom decoys
    "Flats style" of, 21
    Mason factory, 52
    Meldrum's (Tobin) hollow, high-head redhead, *199*
Flyways, xxi, xxiii
Folk art
    decoys as, 6, 12
    Schmidt (Ben) and, 80
Foote, James N., Jr., 16, 17

Geographical area of decoy makers, xxi-xxiii
Goosander
    sheldrake hen by Mason factory, *77, 79*
    sheldrake pair by Mason factory, *64*
Goose
    blue (Schmidt), Plate 1, *103*
    Canada
        hollow (Chambers), *144*
        St. Clair Flats Shooting Co. (maker unknown), *142*
        by Schmidt (Ben), Plate 1, *104, 111*
        by Schmidt (Frank), *107*
        by Schramm, *2*

221. Chambers redhead, early round-head style.

slope-breast (Peterson factory), *66*
two-legged stickup (Wallaceburg, Ontario), *7*
Canada Club, Plates 12-13
    by Chambers, *140*
    by Lincoln, *24*
    by Reeves (John), *145*
    by Ward (David, St. Clair Flats Shooting Co.), *144*

    by Warin, 94, *141*
Gunning decoys
    by Schmidt, Plates 14-15
    by Schroeder, Plates 4-5

Hall, Julie, 2, 24
Hall, Michael, 2
Hamilton, Ontario
    redhead by Morris and, *204*
    redheads by Dalton and, *129*
Harsen's Island (Lake St. Clair)
    bufflehead (South Channel, maker unknown) and, *182*
    Cummings' mallard pair and, *163*
    lowhead whistler (maker unknown) and, *189*
    Pashpatel's black and duck, and *173*
    Unger's redheads and, *35*
Heads. *See also* Highhead style decoy; Lowhead style decoy; Necks; Round-head style decoy; Turned-head style decoy
    Bach's carving and, 42
    Kelson's carving and, 32

222. Redhead of unknown origin.

Quillen's carving and, 17
Schweikart's carving and, 25-26
Unger's carving and, 23
Hen decoys. *See also* Drake decoys
    bluebill (Mason factory), *63, 67, 87*
    bluebill (rounded-head by Chambers), *117*
    bluebill (Schmidt), *108*
    bluebill (two-thirds size by Kellie), *139*
    canvasback (compostition body by Schroeder), *96*
    canvasback (maker unknown), *155*
    canvasback (Reghi), *50, 53*
    lowhead whistler (Schweikart), *27*
    mallard (Kelson), *45*
    mallard (Schmidt), Plates 14-15, *98*
    pintail (Schmidt), Plates 14-15
    Schweikart's painting and, 29
    sheldrake (Mason factory), *77, 79*

Hendrie, George
    mallard by, *172*
    teal pair by, *214*
    Wilson's snipe by, *147*
Heron (Pozzini), *146*
High-head style decoy
    canvasback drake by Schroeder, *97*
    canvasbacks by Peters, *193*
        hollow, *195*
    longneck canvasback (maker unknown), *194*
    redhead by Finkel, *200*
    redhead (hollow) by Tobin Meldrum, *199*
    redheads (maker unknown), *196, 197*
Hollow decoys. *See also* Solid decoys
    black duck (maker unknown), *114*
    bluebill (maker unknown), *217*
    bufflehead drake (Malinski), *4*
    Canada goose (Chambers), *143*
    Canada goose (Peterson factory), *66*
    canvasback drake (McDonald), *25*
    canvasback hen (maker unknown), *155*
    canvasback (high-head, humped-back, Peters), *195*
    canvasback (Schroeder), *94*
    canvasback (snaky-head, St. Clair Flats), *17*
    canvasback (Strubing), *18, 134*
    canvasback (Wells), *130*
    goose (Ward's, St. Clair Flats Shooting Co.), *144*
    high-headed redhead (Tobin Meldrum), *199*
    Quillen's decoys and, 16-17, 89
    redhead (Wells), *131*
    St. Clair Flats Shooting Co. and, 91, 94, 95, 97, *144*
    Schroeder and, 75
    Schweikart's decoys and, 25
    Unger's decoys and, 23
    unpopularity of (after WWI), 74
    whistler drake (Schweikart), *36*
    whistler (Wilkinson), *177*
Hudson, Ira, 31
Hunt clubs. *See also names of specific hunt clubs*
    carving styles and, 25
    historical background on, 88-98
The Huntress (Schweikart yacht), 31
Hydrodynamics
    Schroeder and, 74, 75, 76
    Schweidart and, 30

"JRW Maker," 25
    pintail by, *11*
    St. Clair Flats Shooting Co. and, 91, 96

Kellie, Ed (One Arm)
    bluebill by, *138, 139*
    canvasback by, *136*
    redhead by, *137*
Kelson, James R., 25
    balsa bluebill by, *43*
    balsa canvasback sleeper by, *43*
    balsa redhead by, *46*
    biographical sketch of, 32-35
    mallard drake by, *44*
    mallard hen by, *45*
    Reghi and, 36-40
    Schroeder and, 76
Kelson, Malcomb, 32

Laing, Albert, 25
Lake Erie
    hunting clubs on, 88

as part of geographical area of decoy makers, xxi
whistler (maker unknown) and, *179*
Lake St. Clair. *See also* St. Clair Flats
Cummings's mallard pair and, *163*
decoy styles and, 25
hooded merganser (maker unknown) and, *206*
Meldrum's (Alexander) canvasback drake and, *157*
Meldrum's (Tobin) redhead and, *199*
as part of geographical area of decoy makers, xxi
Reghi and, 40
Lake St. Clair Fishing and Shooting Club (now the Old Club), 88, 89
Lambert, Frank W., 48
Lamerand, Ed, black ducks by, *168*
Leamington, Ontario, hollow whistler (Wilkinson) and, *177*
Lezotte, Edward, 17
Lighthouse Cove, Ontario, hooded merganser (Mailloux) and, *208*
Lincoln, Joe, 24
Logs. *See* Wood used in making decoys
Long Point Bay, lowhead whistler (maker unknown) and, *189*
Long Point Company, Quillen's boat-body decoys and, *29*
Lowhead style decoy
bufflehead, *5*
canvasback, *8*
canvasback by Schweikart, *192*
Chambers' black duck, *121*
Mason factory bluebill, *88*
Mason factory bluebill hen, *67, 87*
Quillen's carving and, 14-16
Quillen's redheads and, *30*
redhead by Smith, *192*
Schroeder's canvasback drake, *97*
Schweikart's canvasback, *39*
studies in Michigan style of (makers unknown), *191*
three uncommon examples of (makers unknown), *190*
whistler (Harsen's Island and Long Point, maker unknown), *189*
whistler (Sampier), *188*

McDonald, Zeke
analysis of canvasback decoys of, 6
black duck by, *174*
hollow canvasback drake by, *25*
redhead by (distinctive head styling), *201*
Mackey, William, 31
Mackey, William J., Jr., 80
Mailloux, Charles, hooded merganser by, *208*
Malinsk, Irving, hollow bufflehead drake by, *4*
Mallard, Plate 16, 94, 95
by Cummings, *163*
drake by Kelson, *44*
drake by Schroeder, Plates 4-5
by Hendrie, *172*
hen by Kelson, *145*
Mason factory, Plates 6-7, *62, 70, 71*
by Schmidt, *100, 101, 102*
hen, Plates 14-15, *98*
Marine City
DeCoe's canvasbacks and, *153*
Strubing's canvasbacks and, *18, 134*
Mason factory, 91
analysis of, 51-52, 56
bluebill, *63, 86*
hen, *87*
lowhead, *67, 88*
bluewing teal, Plates 6-7, *72*
buffleheads, *75*
canvasback, Plates 6-7, *64, 81, 82, 83, 152*
coot, Plates 6-7, *78*
greenwing teal, *74*
instability of decoys and, 21
mallard, Plates 6-7, *62, 70, 71*
pintail, Plates 6-7
Pointe Mouillee Club and, 17
sheldrake hen, *77, 79*
sheldrake pair, *76*
shorebird, Plate 11
solid wood duck, *80*
widgeon, Plates 6-7, *69*
drake, *68*
Mason, Herbert W., 52
Mason, William J., 48, 49, 51-52, 89

223. A pintail drake from Larry Hayden's hunting rig.

Meldrum, Alexander (Yock), canvasback drake by, 122
Meldrum, Tobin
    canvasback high-head by, *198*
    hollow, flat-bottomed, high-head redhead by, *199*
Merganser
    American (Christie brothers), *207*
    Dodge factory, *85*
    hooded (Lake St. Clair, maker unknown), *206*
    hooded (Mailloux), *208*
    sheldrake hen by Mason factory, *77, 79*
    sheldrake pair by Mason factory, *76*
Meyer, Joe, black duck by, *166*
Middle Channel, Unger's cottage and, 20
Misch, Otto
    canvasback by, *133*
    whistler by, *132*
Mitchells Bay, 96
    Meyer's black duck and, *166*
Monhegan Island, Unger's decoys and, 23
Monroe, Kellie's canvasbacks and, *136, 139*
Monroe Marsh Club, 88
Morris, John, redhead by, *204*
Mount Clemens, Michigan
    carving styles and, 25
    Vandenboesch's turned-head canvasback and, *148*

Necks. *See also* Bullneck style decoy; Heads
    Kelson's carving and, 32
    longneck decoys and, *193-200*
    Quillen's carving and, 14-15, 17
New Baltimore, Canada goose decoy and, *2*
Newberry, Truman H., 96

O'Brien, Donal C., Jr., xxi
The Old Club (formerly Lake St. Clair Fishing and Shooting Club), 88, 89

Painting. *See also* Combing (painting technique)
    Bach and, 42
    canvasback decoy analysis and, 5
    Quillen and, 16
    Schroeder and, 75
    Schweikart and, 29
    scratch (Wells), *130*
    as Strubing's trademark, 19
    Unger and, 23
Pashpatel, Leo, black duck by, *173*
Pearl Beach
    bufflehead by Sampier and, *185*
    redhead by Tobin Meldrum and, *199*
Peterson factory, 91
    analysis of, 48-49, 51
    bluewing teal, *73*
    slope-breast Canada, *66*
Peterson, George, 48
Peters, Scott
    high-head canvasback by, *193*
    high-head, humped-back canvasback by, *195*
Pintail, Plate 16, 95
    by Chambers, *127*
    Dodge factory, *84*
    drake by Schmidt, Plates 14-15, *106*
    drake by Warin, *125, 128*
    hen by Schmidt, Plates 14-15
    "JRW Maker," *11*
    Mason factory, Plates 6-7
    pair by Schmidt, *99*
    Port Rowan (maker unknown), *120*
    by Quillen, *32*
    by Reeves (Phineas), *123*
    by Smith (Chris), *3*
Pirnie, Miles, widgeon by, *1*
Pointe Mouillee Shooting Club, 88, 89-91
    Mason factory decoys and, 17
    Quillen and, 14, 16, 17
Port Huron, black duck (Finch) and, *171*
Port Rowan, Ontario
    goose (John Reeves) and, *145*
    pintail (maker unknown) and, *120*
    pintail (Phineas Reeves) and, *123*
    Quillen's boat-body decoys and, 29
Pozzini, Charlie, heron by, *146*
Price of Chambers' canvasbacks, 24
Puddle duck, Unger's tail differences and, 34

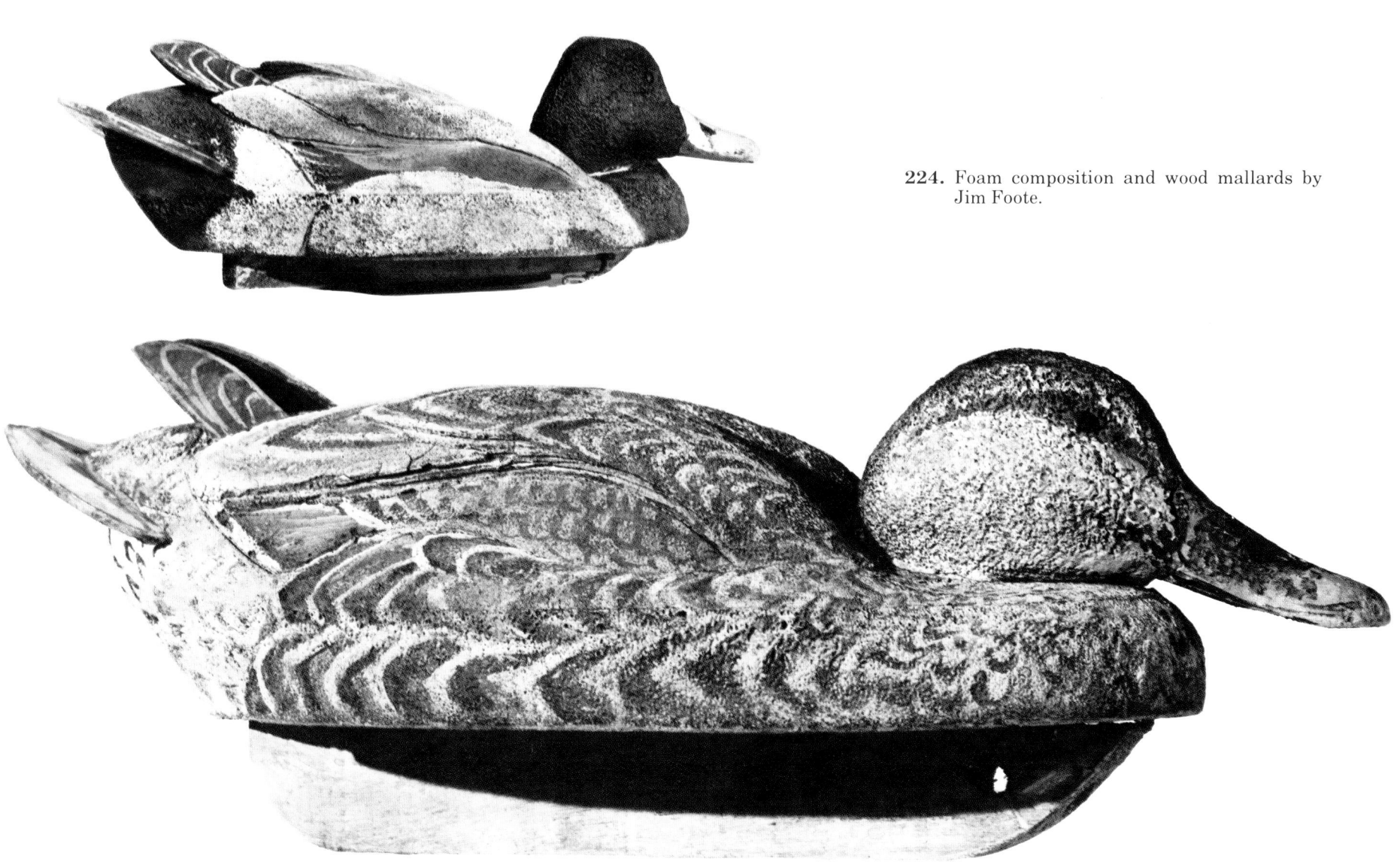

224. Foam composition and wood mallards by Jim Foote.

Purdo, Nick
    balsa canvasback heads of (on Ben Schmidt's decoys), *209*
    redhead balsa by, *210*
    Reghi and, *36*

Quillen, Nate, *xxiii*, *91*
    biographical sketch of, *14-19*
    bluebill by, *28*
    bluewing teal decoys by, Plate 10
    boat-body style and, *28, 29*
    pintail by, *32*
    Pointe Mouillee Shooting Club and, *89*
    redhead decoys by, Plate 10, *28, 29, 30, 31*
    widgeon drake by, *31*

Redhead
    by Bach, *42, 60, 61*
    balsa by Purdo, *210*
    by Dalton, *129*
    drake by Chambers, *126*
    drake ("Flats Club," maker unknown), *205*
    high-head (Finkel), *200*
    high-head, hollow, flat-bottomed (Tobin Meldrum), *199*
    by Kellie, *137*
    Kelson's balsa, *46*
    lowhead (C.C. Smith Co.), *192*
    by McDonald, *201*
    by Morris, *204*
    by Quillen, Plate 10
        boat-body style and, *28, 29*
        body style and, *31*
        lowhead, *30*
    "St. Clair Flats Long-neck," *197*

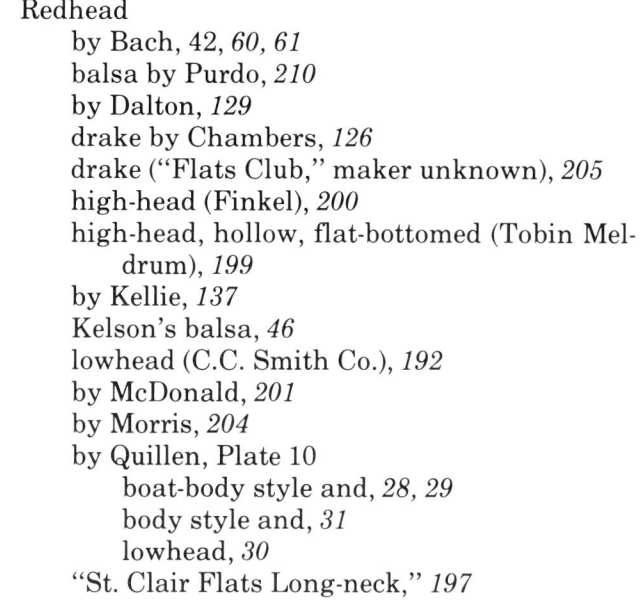

225. Two old redhead decoys from the Canada Club, c. 1890.

by Schroeder, Plates 4-5, 74, *89, 95*
by Schweikart, 25, 31, *41*
sleeper (maker unknown), *203*
by C.C. Smith Co., *192, 202*
by Unger, *35*
    analysis of, 21-23
by Warin, *119*
by Wells, *131*
Reeves family, 25
Reeves, John, 91
    goose by, *145*
Reeves, Phineas, pintail by, *123*
Reghi, Ralph, 25
    biographical sketch of, 36-41
    bluebill drake by, *46*
    canvasbacks by, Plate 8, *47, 49*
        analysis of, 5
        bullneck, *14, 16, 52*
        hen, *50, 53*
        rasp marks and, *49*
    Kelson and, 32-34
    redhead drake by, *51*
    Schroeder and, 76
Ringbill, 95
    by Baumgartner, *215*
    by Schroeder, Plates, 4-5, 74
    by Warin, *118*
Round-head style decoy, Chambers' bluebill hen, *117*
Ruddy
    by Schmidt (Frank), *12*
    by Schroeder, Plates 4-5

Saginaw Bay area, whistler (Misch) and, *132*
St. Anne's Club, sleeper canvasback and, 6-7, *27*
St. Clair Flats. *See also* Lake St. Clair
    bluebill decoy (Dodge factory) and, 54
    canvasback and, *9*
    Dodge and Mason decoys and, 21
    hollow canvasback (maker unknown) and, *149*
    long-neck redhead and, *197*
    McDonald's black duck and, *174*
    as part of geographical area of decoy makers, xxi, xxiii
    St. Anne's sleeper canvasback and, *27*
    Schweikart's decoys and, 25
    swan decoy and, Plate 9
    whistler (maker unknown) and, *180*
St. Clair Flats Shooting Co.
    black duck (Chambers) and, *124*
    goose (John Reeves) and, *145*
    goose (maker unknown) and, *142*
    historical background on, 91-97
    hollow black duck (maker unknown) and, *114*
    hollow canvasback (Wells) and, *130*
    hollow redhead (Wells) and, *131*
    redhead drake (maker unknown) and, *205*
    redhead (Warin) and, *119*
    swan decoy (maker unknown) and, *6*
    teal pair (Hendrie) and, *214*
St. Clair Flats Shooting Company, Ltd. (*also known as* Canada Club, Toronto Club), 88
    goose decoys of, Plates 12-13
    Hendrie's Wilson's snipe and, *147*
St. Clair River, whistler by Strubing and, *135*
Sampier, Budgeon
    bufflehead by, *185*
    canvasback by, *160*
    whistler (lowhead) by, *188*
Schmidt, Ben
    biographical sketch of, 80-87
    black duck by, *110, 169*
    bluebill hen by, *108*
    blue goose by, Plate 1, *103, 105*
    Canada goose by, Plate 1, *104, 111*
    canvasback by, *15*
        analysis of, 5
    mallard hen by, Plates, 14-15, *98*
    mallards by, *100, 101, 102*
    pintail drake by, *106*
    pintail pair by, *99*
    Schroeder and, 76
    whistler drake by, *10*
Schmidt, Frank
    biographical sketch of, 86
    black duck by, *112*
    bluebill by, *109*
    bufflehead by, *183*

226. Canada goose by Frank Schmidt.

    Canada goose by, *107*
    ruddy by, *12*
Schramm, Butch, Canada goose by, *2*
Schroeder, Tom
    biographical sketch of, 72-79
    black duck by, *169*
    bluebill by, *93*
    box-bottom canvasback by, *90*
    box-bottom redhead by, *89*
    canvasback by, *91, 92, 94*
        drake, *97*
        hen, *96*
    gunning decoys by, Plates 4-5
    redhead (composition body) by, *95*
    skirt-bottom canvasback by, *92*
Schweikart, Carl, 30-31
Schweikart family, 20
Schweikart, John, xxii, 76
    biographical sketch of, 24-31
    canvasbacks by, Plates 2-3
        aluminum wing tip, *37, 38*
        analysis of, 6
        lowhead, *192*
        tin-wing, *13*
    coot by, *42*
    redhead by, *41*
    whistlers by, Plates 2-3
        drake, *40*
        hollow, *36*
Schweikart, Walter, 30
Schweikart, Walter, Jr., 30
Scriven, Danny, whistler by, *178*
Shelbourne Museum (Vermont)
    catalogue of, 89, 95
    Schroeder decoys and, 79
Sheldrake
    hen by Mason factory, *77, 79*
    pair by Mason factory, *76*
Shorebird decoys (Mason factory), Plate 11
Shoveler duck, pair by Wells, xxiii
Skirt-bottom decoys by Schroeder, 76, *92*
Sleeper style decoy
    canvasback by Zachmann, *26*
    Kelson's balsa decoys and, *43*
    redhead (maker unknown), *203*

Smith, Chris, pintail decoy by, *3*
Smith Co. *See* C.C. Smith Co.
Snipe. *See* Wilson's snipe
Solid decoys. *See also* Hollow decoys
    Bach and, 42
    bluebill (Schroeder), *93*
    drake wood duck (Mason factory), *80*
    Quillen and, 16, 89
    ringbill (Warin), *118*
    Schroeder and, 74
Sorenson, Hal, 42
South Channel, bufflehead (pre-Civil War) and, *5*
Steiner, Thomas, black duck by, *162*
Stevens, Harvey A., 48
Stratford, Unger's decoys and, 23
Strawberry Island
    biographical sketch of Schweikart and, 25, 30
    Schroeder and, 76
    Schweikart's bullneck canvasback and, *37*
Strubing, Walter
    canvasbacks by, *18, 19, 134*
        analysis of, 5
    whistler by, *135*
Style. *See also* names of specific decoy styles, e.g.,
        Bullneck style decoy, Feeding style decoy,
        Sleeper style decoy, *etc.*
    Bach's early, *55, 56, 59, 61*
    carving schools and, 25
    decoys as folk art and, 6, 12, 80
    of Dodge factory, 49
        flared headfeathers and, *85*
    heads on McDonald redheads and, *201*
    Kelson's, *43*
    Lamerand's meticulous, *168*
    pinched neck canvasback, *20*
    Quillen's, *31*
        boat-body, *28, 29*
    Reghi's rasp marks and, *49*
    Schmidt (Ben) and, 80
    Schroeder's, 74
    Schweikart's aluminum wing tips and, *37, 38*
    Stratford (Wheeler), 72
    Unger's
        analysis of, 21-23
        tail differences in, *34*

    Walpole (of George Warin), 20
Swan
    St. Clair Flats decoy of, Plate 9
    St. Clair Flats Shooting Co. decoy of, *6,* 96-97
Swanson, Ronald S., 20, 72

Teal
    balsa pair by Hendrie, *214*
    bluewing
        balsa by Finch, *213*
        factory, Plates 6-7, *72, 73*
        by Quillen, Plate 10
        by Schroeder, Plates 4-5
    greenwing
        drake by Schmidt, Plates 14-15
        Mason factory, *74*
        by Schroeder, Plates 4-5
Tin-wing canvasback (Schweikart), *13*
Tip-up decoy (black duck, maker unknown), *167*
Tom Run (area), canvasback by Crooks and, *151*
Tools
    of Bach, 42
    of Kelson and Reghi, 33
    rasp marks (Reghi) and, *49*
Toronto Club (*also known as* St. Clair Flats
        Shooting Company, Ltd.), 88
    goose decoys of, Plates 12-13
    Hendrie's Wilson's snipe and, *147*
Torrey, Harry N., 91
Turned-head style decoy
    Bach's black duck, *59*
    Cummings's black duck, *165*
    Kelson's, *46*
    Mason factory bluebill, *63*
    Reghi's, *46*
    Vandenboesch's canvasback, *148*
Two-legged stickup decoy (Canada goose), *7*

Unger, Charles J.
    biographical sketch of, 20-23
    black duck by, *34*
    canvasback by, *33, 34*
    redhead by, *35*
Unger, Frederick C., 20-21

Vandenboesch, Ted, turned-head canvasback by, *148*
Variegated plumage
    sheldrake hen by Mason factory and, *77, 79*
    sheldrake pair by Mason factory and, *76*

Wallaceburg, Ontario, two-legged stickup Canada goose and, 7
Wallach, Carl, 25
    analysis of decoys of, 7
    bobtailed canvasback by, *21*
Walpole Island Indian band, 98
Ward, David (of Toronto)
    canvasback by, *150*
    St. Clair Flats Shooting Co. and, 91-94
    St. Clair Flats Shooting Co. hollow goose by, *144*
Ward, Lem, 5, 29
Warin family, 25
Warin, George, xxiii
    decoys by, Plate 16
    goose by, *141*
    pintail drake by, *128*
    redhead by, *119*
    ringbill by, *118*
    St. Clair Flats Shooting Co. and, 91, 94, 95, 96
    Unger decoys and, 20
    as Ward's (David) shooting partner, *144*
Warin, James, 91, 96
Wells, John R.
    decoys by, Plate 16
    hollow canvasback by, *130*
    hollow redhead by, *131*
    St. Clair Flats Shooting Co. and, 91, 94, 96
    shoveler pair by, xxiii
Wheeler, Shaing, 72
Whistler
    high-domed (Lake Erie, maker unknown), *179*
    hollow (Wilkinson), *177*
    Lake Erie drake (maker unknown), *176*
    lowhead (Sampier), *188*
    by Misch, 132
    St. Clair Flats (maker unknown), *180*
    by Schmidt, *10*
    by Schweikart, Plates 2-3, 25, 27
        hollow, *36*
    by Scriven (lower Detroit river bobtail), *178*
    by Strubing, *135*
Whitmore Lake, 74
Widgeon
    drake by Mason factory, *68*
    drake by Quillen, *31*
    feeding pose (Pirnie), *1*
    Mason factory, Plates 6-7, *69*
    by Schmidt, Plates 14-15
Wilkinson, Russ, hollow whistler by, *177*
Wilson's snipe (Hendrie), *147*
Wood duck
    by Chambers, Plate 16
    Mason factory, *80*
Wood used in making decoys
    cedar (Quillen), 16
    cedar telephone poles (Bach), 42
    Kelson and Reghi and, 33
    sugar pine (Bach's heads), 42

Zachmann, John
    canvasbacks by
        analysis of, 12
        gigantic sized, *152*
        sleeper, *26*
    Reghi and, 36
Zembke, Felix, 17

227. A very rare J. Dodge whistler decoy, c. 1900.

Text design and layout by Lowell G. Jackson.

Keylining and assembly by Graphic House, Inc.

Production coordination and design of dust jacket and endpapers by Frederick Associates.

Color separations, duotones, and lithography by Litho-Art, Inc.

Lithographed on Vintage Velvet and Vintage Gloss Enamel from Northwest Paper Division of Potlatch Corporation.

Bound with Holliston Record Buckram cloth by Riverside Book Bindery, Inc.